THE MODERN
ARTIST
AND
SONGWRITER
JOURNAL AND TOOLKIT

**A WORKBOOK WITH EVERYTHING
YOU NEED FOR A CAREER CREATING
MUSIC IN TODAY'S MUSIC INDUSTRY**

Written and Compiled By

BLAKE MAKES MUSIC

ROCK MY RECORDS

WHAT DO YOU LISTEN TO?

For Eliana Rey Carpenter. Do great things and may the force be with you.

Love, Dad.

The Modern Artist and Songwriter Journal and Toolkit by Blake Makes Music

Published by Rock My Records

https://rockmyrecords.com/
http://musicadvice.io/
https://blakemakesmusic.com/

Cover by Blake Makes Music

First Edition 2021

A WORD OF HONESTY
What are you selling me here?
I choose to be upfront about my intentions with this book.

You will see multiple mentions to my website throughout this book. The website, MusicAdvice.io is meant to be an extension of your experience while reading and learning this effective music productivity method. Everything that is offered directly from me is 100% free, except for one service (which I will mention later). There is even a good chance that you got this book for free or extremely cheap, if it's digital. If you paid for it, it's most likely in-print or because the distributor of the digital versions didn't let me select $0 for some reason. If any money is made from this book in print, it went to cover printing costs. I have chosen to forgo much income directly from this book, and have decided to mostly make income on the backend of this experience you are about to partake in.

I use tactics from this book in my own music career, and in no way exaggerate any of the results or make any promises. I like to help other musicians succeed, but I also like to work for myself. I encourage you to work for yourself as well. It's extremely freeing. My goal for you is to build something on your own. I will give you the treasure map, but the journey is yours.

The site mentioned throughout this book will take you to a landing page with a bunch of different resources. Some of the links are my socials, content, channels, and stores. Many of them are my own links, but some of them are what are called affiliate links. These links will sometimes provide a discount to a subscription, service or product. Every affiliate link there though is a product that I use myself and there are no links there to products that I do not use personally. I only recommend products that I use myself. When you use these links, it will sometimes give you a discount as well as provide me with a tiny commission at no additional cost to you. For that, I appreciate you.

Behind this book is a very accessible and real person.
THE ART OF FREE

This book is as inexpensive as I could make it, my content is free, connecting with me is free. I am writing this book to help extend my audience online. It is my hope that you see value in what you have gained from these pages, and interact with me in some way online.

I make income from this book by you interacting with me on other platforms. Those platforms are still free to use but it would greatly help me grow my audience. I am not trying to take over the world or anything, but I do believe my messages can help a lot of new and even seasoned music makers. We all have the dream and we can all learn from one another. As my community of people like you grow, I make income from the ads on my YouTube channel, my Twitch streams, the podcast, and things like my Patreon. Also, I have some pretty awesome merch available too, but that is for my ride or die fans. I believe that the information and community we build is important, and that's why its always free. if you need to connect with me and my content on a more personal level, I do have a pretty awesome Patreon page. I only expect 1-5% of you to take advantage of that source, but it is pretty awesome. There, I offer you a TON of goodies to help your music career. But again, I am still available to you though Twitch, YouTube, Instagram, Discord, my Podcast and much more. Hey join me online and I'll help you build a Patreon, too!

If you have appreciated anything I show you, I just ask that you tell your friends about it. You can do this through social media and/or even leaving this book a good review wherever you got it from. It would be extremely helpful and even more appreciated. My goal is to create an amazing community of music makers just like you and I who can count on one another to succeed. I have many plans after this book and will always share the benefits with my audience. The more music makers in this community, the better. I sincerely appreciate you!

ABOUT THE AUTHOR
Who is this guy anyway?
Why you should take advice from Blake Makes Music

My name is Blake Carpenter. You can find me everyone online under, Blake Makes Music. Why that name? Well because my name is common, and there are even a few musicians out there with the same name as me. To make life easier, I decided to just go with that. Plus, it sounds cool, right? Meh, well I think so. I have been making music since 1999 when I was only a kid. I have been writing songs, playing in bands, and doing the whole thing. I made a LOT of mistakes trying to figure out how to navigate the music industry during that time. I then went to school for audio engineering at a community college and later for guitar performance at Musician's Institute. I got good education, paid a lot of money, and all the knowledge took years to solidify in my mind.

I made some connections, worked on various music projects, and eventually actually started to make some money. From all the money that I spent in college, the biggest thing that I learned came from Ritch Esra. He taught a couple of music business classes at Musician's Institute. He said, "There are tens of thousands of musicians in the United States, all making income making music... and you don't know who they are." That blew my mind! It made sense though! My idea of success was being rich and famous, but there are an infinite number of possibilities between that and failure. I started to think about how I remember all these indie bands, songwriters, and composers just in the city of Houston who all did a few awesome things or had a small but dedicated following. Of course, they were paying their bills. I started to see music differently at that point. Mind you, this still before streaming services, Patreon and modern YouTube channels. I went through cycles of create, fail, repeatedly and eventually figured out a path for myself as a music maker.

I then later got a job working with music students at a large private college. I worked with music production students as a career advisor, helping them get their resumes, portfolios, and plans together for working in the industry and being their short-term mentor. I didn't just have a lot of students; I had a LOT of students. I mean THOUSANDS. They all came to me for help and guidance, which was awesome! I soon realized working with people younger than myself, that they for the most part had a lot of the same issues. They were all afraid to make music because they thought they weren't good enough yet. Yet here they are, spending $30k-60k learning how to produce music and they were all afraid to make it. The mindset was all wrong. They were getting so much information in school, that they couldn't even keep it organized.

I soon began approaching that job in a different way. I started making road maps and charts everyone and drew out paths with checklists and to-dos. I started working with students on their portfolios similarly to how financial advisors work with investments. Then it hit me. My epiphany. Combine financial market strategies with the new music industry strategies. My concept worked like this... If you knew for a fact you could make only $1 a month from each song you finished and released, how many songs do you need make to pay your bills? Now make that many songs. Then release them.

4

ABOUT THE AUTHOR
Your music is a financial asset
Why you should take advice from Blake Makes Music

Your music is a tangible and real asset. Its only worthless if you keep it on your computer or in a notebook. So, they listened to me, and it worked! I had cut 5 to 10 years of failure out for them. I figured out the formula. It was simple. Make as much music as you possibly can, release it in the right way, promote it to the right people and start back over. Next song, new day, move on. Plus, it makes you a better songwriter, musician, and producer.

It's not about you as an artist or producer, it's about your catalog. Don't be silly, only you care about yourself that much. Your listeners care about your music. Your songs are like financial assets so think of songs like penny stocks that pay you dividends every month. Worthless now, but if you have a lot of them and you put some work behind them later, and they will increase in value. Now those songs pay you more than $1 a month, and your fanbase and output grows exponentially. The good news for you, is that songs usually pay in the form of passive income. The bad news about passive income is that it always takes time to build your music system up! That's okay, we have time if we have anything, right? Soon the value of your songs will go from $1 a month to maybe thousands a month per song per month. You should view your catalog of music as a collective. An average value. For example, you own a store selling baseball cards, you wouldn't measure your success by measuring the success of card. At the end of the day, you'd measure success by calculating the entire profit of the entire store each day, week, month and year. Don't put your music on a pedestal. Your music is no different than the baseball card store. The way to raise your "music value" (or your product) is by connecting with more fans and making those connections deeper.

"It can't be that simple." Yes, it is. Of course, there are some things you need to do with the song and how you go about selling your music and generating new fans, but for the most part it's straight forward.

I later started taking my concepts and compiling them together into an online business helping more musicians outside of my job. I mapped out my system as a podcast model. I started the podcast, Blake Makes Music. It's not just a podcast, it's an education system, a music eco-system and a productivity hack! Why spend all that money going to school for music, when I can just give you the success shortcuts now, and you can thank me later? Okay cool because I thought that sounded good too. Don't worry, I turned what is a complex industry into a super simple method. You can get more from me at www.musicadvice.io

My name is Blake, and I am a Music Career Advisor. Nice to meet you, I can't wait to help you!

Some Albums

AN ILLUMINATI JOKE

REACHING OUT TO ME
HOW I CAN HELP YOU AFTER THIS BOOK
Let's be friends, join my community of music makers!

I take an interactive approach with my readers, fans, or musicians who want some extra guidance. I have put together a great ecosystem to connect with you in the way that you prefer! Connect with me how you want, send me a message, participate in the videos, ask me questions for the podcast!

All of the platforms to connect with me on MusicAdvice.io
1. Twitch Live Stream Q&A, Its a party!
2. Discord - Chat with me and members directly.
3. Reddit community where you can get community advice.
4. My Music Club Subscription on Rock My Records
5. The Blake Makes Music Website
6. Podcast where I give advice on topics and review your songs
7. YouTube Videos that cover specific topics suggested by you!
8. All Social Media Platforms (Facebook, Instagram, TikTok, Twitter, LinkedIn)
9. Mailing List - Useful tips, news and other things for your career
10. Voicemail to ask questions on the podcast

What is MusicAdvice.io?

Musicadvice.io is a landing page for all of my content. We all have a lot of links to our various social media pages and this is a site for mine. There, I offer extensions to this book, affiliate links to products that help you manage your music career. I also have all kinds of links there to help you succeed.

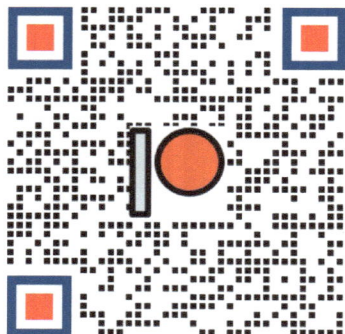

SCAN ME

SCAN ME

WANT MORE JOURNAL PAGES?
I have them available for print
I know that you may need some more of these amazing journal pages. I have them available for subscribers on my Patreon with some other amazing things.

What else is on my Patreon?
Music contacts, start guides, give-aways, a phone call to say thanks, suggest topics for the show, voting rights, all my music, special videos, Zoom meetings, music feedback, special access to me and bunch of other cool things! Go check it out!

HOW TO USE THIS BOOK

What's going on in this thing?

Rip it out, pin it up!

I actually started to use these pages for myself and realized that there are probably a lot of other songwriters out there who need some help managing their productivity. So let me give you the rundown before you get started. Make sure that you check out the entire book before you go on your new productive songwriting journey.

The Journal Pages

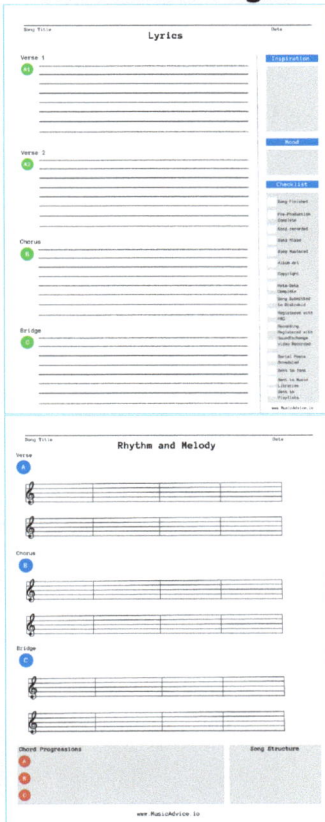

Use these two pages to help you organize and write your songs. These are designed to be front and back for each song. There are enough sheets in here to write a song a week, just like the example plan. I would recommend using pencil on these, and put these on your wall or store them in a binder for later.

The Split Sheets

These are called "split-sheets". You can use this when you are writing music with others. You will need this typically before the process of writing. Its awkward bringing this up after the session is done, so make sure you all agree to fill this out before you write. The instructions are straight forward, make copies and send to all songwriters. There are a few copies to get you started.

The Calendar Pages

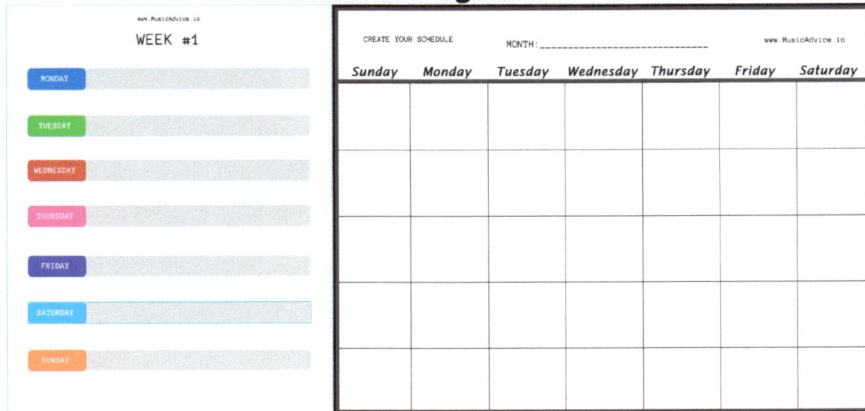

This is your calendar. You should rip these out and put them on your walls. Use pencil on these, as plans change. But you should really get on a role if you stick to the plan. It may be difficult at first, but that is normal. It's all based on doing something productive every day, big or small but keeping yourself accountable. If you are writing with a partner, create your schedules together. Break your year down, your month, weeks and days.

THE METHODOLOGY
Getting better means getting more efficient
Don't be afraid to write a bad song.

Most of the time when I talk to new music makers, they usually tell me the same things. That they're trying to find their sound, that they don't have the skills yet, and that they are waiting for an opportunity. They also follow up with the fact that they don't have a lot of music yet. Sometimes I will hear an aspiring songwriter tell me that they have lots of lyrics, but no recorded music.

So, that's not going to work for you anymore. Sorry friend. You need to be able to get these 'bad songs' out of your system. The only way to become a better songwriter is to just write more songs, consistently. More importantly, you need to do this on a schedule and a plan, without feeling like you're writing dumb songs. Because even though you may feel like you are writing a dumb song when it's forced, you're not.

The 'cranking' out music method is writing as many songs as you possibly can, and timing yourself based on availability. For example, if you write one song a day and you only have two hours of free time, then you need to write and record your demo in two hours. That sounds crazy, I know. But trust me, you will thank me later. Yes, your first time you will probably get a song that you do not like.

If you have more time or a different goal in mind, your plan may be different. Maybe your goal is to write one song a week? Great! Every week, write then record then release.

But, look at it this way. Most professional songwriters are pushing out 3 - 4 songs a day when working on music. That is where your competition is. So the best way to get to that point is to process songwriting like you would if you were going to the gym. You don't go to gym only when you feel like it or feel inspired. You will never lose weight or get healthier with that mentality. Plus your body would be super confused. You go on a schedule and with a plan. As you get started, you will feel like you don't 'want' to go to gym. But after a few consistent weeks, it gets easier. Slowly but surely you get better and better at what exercises you are doing as well as eventually liking to go. Its a slow consistent game. This method is like your personal trainer for creativity.

Creativity is like a muscle and if you do not use it, you lose it. I have experienced creative atrophy. It sucks. It's also known as writers block. The good news is that natural born talent doesn't matter when taking this approach, and any strong willed person can at least become a decent songwriter.

So, pick a schedule and stick to it. You start your journey by working backwards. Start with a goal. The goal sheets are included in the book as well. Let's say you want to write and release 12 songs this year. Great! Thats only one a month.

Now, let's break that down. What do you have to make that happen? You write for a week. Record for a week, do your admin work for a week and then release and promote for a week. Easy!

I know this all sounds good, but are you ready for the scary part? I want you to release these songs to the world. DEPENDING on your goals, releasing may mean different things. So let me break down for you what that means for each person and why it's important to release the music in certain ways to 'finish' the song.

THE METHODOLOGY
Continued...
What to do with your songs and how to finish them.

So your songs are like your personal little children. I know. It's hard to let them go. But you're going to have to let them leave the nest. The good news is that you will never be an 'empty nester' because if you are doing what you are supposed to, you will continue to write more songs.

Most artists struggle with finishing music. They write parts of a song, and get bored or stop being inspired, and move on to the next track. The problem with this is that they end up with a portfolio with nothing. Also, most people who say they will return to the song later, never do. Because we are creatives. That's how our mind works. But the creative mindset is rarely the productive one. The good news is that you can train your mind to do many things, creative productivity is one of them.

Since finishing the song is so important, let's define what finish means.

For the singer songwriter, also known as an artist. Finishing a song means that you write the entire song, record it and release it to the masses. Those songs are yours. Sitting on them does you absolutely no good. Releasing music for artists will be defined as putting the songs out on **streaming** platforms. I do not mean just put it out on SoundCloud. Soundcloud has a good place in the industry, but your goal as an artist is to get a fanbase over the course of time. For that, you need to put your music where the people are. At the time of this writing, the largest music discovery platform is Spotify. You could make the argument for YouTube as well. However, best thing to do is to release your music on streaming platforms **as well as** YouTube. If you want to be an artist and make income...It's not about you or how you feel about where it should go. It's about being where your fans are and converting them to listeners and eventually some of them to customers.

Here is the good news, you can release music these days and then remove it later. You used to not be able to do that. Your songs should be seen as bait to fish for a new audience member. As a singer-songwriter, this is the only way you eat. Also, your music is has copyright once it's in a fixed form.

Releasing music to your audience, even when you have no audience members is extremely important. As always you can get a discount on distribution through Distrokid as well as ask me how to market your brand new release by visiting the site www.musicadvice.io

What about if you write songs, but you're not a performer? Great! We have a solution for you too. You need to write, record, release as well. BUT for you, the release will be defined as putting your finished demos on to Disco.AC in playlists, based on genres. The reason for this is that this is typically how A&R reps from publishing companies want to accept your music. They also want to make sure that the song is not released before they shop it out to artists that they work with.

It's probably a good idea to copyright your music as a collection through the copyright.gov site first before moving on to sending it to these people though. Just as another layer of protection.

You create lists of contacts who accept music (you can ask me how by going to my site musicadvice.io, if you want) and then its considered released once it's sent out and in your Disco Library. This is now a sales game of trying to shop your collection of music out to those who may want it. The "shotgun" marketing technique though isn't the best way. You want to establish relationships with the people before you just send it in blindly. You will also get ghosted and a bunch of "No thanks" but all you need is ONE yes.

THE METHODOLOGY
This one is for everyone.
Getting you music in to Film/TV/Commercials/Video Games/Videos

What about the other option? Yes the other option. Music libraries. If you want your music in film and TV and you don't want to worry too much about live performance, you can also solicit your music to music libraries.

What the heck is that? Long story short, it's a place for content creators to go for "stock music". It works the same way as most stock photo libraries.

Ewww, stock music? Yes. Stock music. Don't knock it until you have tried it! The quality of music in these libraries will surprise you! Also, this is where the money is now days as well as a lot of the exposure for artists. I could and should probably write a whole other book on this business, but I will try to give you the broad bullet points.

If you are an artist or someone who can perform but doesn't want to this is a good and recommended outlet for you. If you are a songwriter who can't perform, then all you need is a musician buddy to operate in this lane. So if that's you, go make friends. Friends are important in this industry too. Even if you are shy, you can go make internet friends.

If you go visit a music library such as https://www.apmmusic.com/ you will get it. You can search hundreds of thousands of songs based on mood, genre, feel, vibe, use, lyrics, tempo, key, etc. So as someone who is creating a quick ad for YouTube or something, this is a great one stop shop for that person to get the right license needed to broadcast your music. Also, you get paid on when and how it's used. All libraries are a little different, and there are A LOT of them. But this system can be navigated as well if you are a songwriter.

This is a numbers game.

The more music you have in a library, the higher chances you have of getting a placement in one of these mediums. There are a lot of legal questions that can be answered through contacting me on my site, MusicAdvice.io but basically you can expect these libraries to take up to HALF of what you earn. That is normal. If anyone asks for more, run.

Some libraries will split the initial fee with you, and then let you keep all of the writers share, and half the publishing. Thats a fair deal. However, these libraries are very competitive and so a lot of them do different things. That doesn't mean it's a scam though. Also, libraries will typically sign a song to their catalog, not a composer or writer. So you can typically have more than one deal with different songs in different libraries. Long story short again, you will need to know two phrases about music libraries.

If a library offers your track a non-exclusive deal this means...
You can shop the same song to other libraries who are also non-exclusive. So you could possibly have the same song in 10 non-exclusive libraries.

If a library offers your track an exclusive deal this means...
You are ONLY allowed to have your song in their library. You are not allowed to use any other means to license your song to other publishing or library companies.

There are pros and cons to each setup. Both are fine. If you want more help on this, ask. But for you, the word "release" will be defined as... in a music library. You will have more success by using the Disco platform to shop your music out to libraries, as this is becoming the standard for music supervisors to use in order to find music for projects. You will also need to create a list and SELL your songs to the right libraries. Lucky for you... I know a few!

THE CUE SHEET
What your songs look like behind the screen
Learn youngling. Learn.

What is a cue sheet? After your music gets put into film or TV, the music coordinator for the show needs to fill this out to send to ASCAP, BMI, and SESAC. It tells them what songs were used and how.

An accurately filled out cue sheet is a log of all the music used in a production. This information includes:

- Series/Film Title
- Series/Film Title AKA
- Episode Title
- Episode Title AKA
- Episode Number
- Air Date
- Show Length
- Music Length
- Production Company Information
- Song/Cue Title
- Composer
- Publisher
- Performing rights society
- Timing
- Usage

USAGE CODES

BI - Background Instrumental
BV - Background Vocal
VI - Visual Instrumental (on camera instrumental performance)
VV - Visual Vocal (on camera vocal performance)
MT - Main Theme
ET - End Title Theme
Logo - Company Logo

ASCAP, BMI AND SESAC will then pay their songwriters based on how many estimated viewers or listeners a show will have and pay out percentage of dues from their fees that the production company paid the PRO for a blanket license to use their PRO catalog. Songs categorized such as "Main Theme" will get paid more than a background instrumental or company logo use.

THE CUE SHEET

What your songs look like behind the screen

Learn youngling. Learn.

Courtesy of BMI.

Some weird adult swim show title, "The one with the cue sheet"

Music Cue Sheet

Cue Sheet Classification: Original
Date Prepared: 12/12/21

Initial Airdate: 1/1/22
Category: Cartoon Series
Version: Cable
Network/Source: Cartoon Network

Program/Show Duration: 18 min. 15 sec.
Total Music Duration: 4 min. 37 sec. (auto calc.)

Program (series, film, etc.) Title: Some weird adult swim show title
Program Title AKA(s): N/A
Episode Title: "The one with the cue sheet"
Episode Title AKA(s): "Cat goes to the bank"
Episode Number: 205
Production Number: 12

Production Company: Telecat Cartoon Space
Mailing Address: 1234 Idedair Thumbwar St, Los Dirty Town, CA 90028
Cue Sheet Prepared By: Angela Smirkle
Email Address: TelecasCartoonProductions@CN.com

Usage Codes: BI = Background Instrumental | BV = Background Vocal | VI = Visual Instrumental | VV = Visual Vocal | MT = Main Title Theme | ET = End Title Theme | Logo

Seq. #	Cue Title (Song/Track Name)	Usage	Time In (optional) h mm ss	Time Out (optional) h mm ss	Duration min. sec.	Role	Composer/Writer First (and Middle) Name	Composer/Writer Last Name	Publisher Name	PRO Affiliation	% Shares
1	Freak Zone	MT	0 00 00	0 00 30	0 30	Composer	Johan Janey	Johnson		ASCAP	100.00%
			0 00 00	0 00 30	0 30	Publisher			Pinicle Pint Publishing	ASCAP	100.00%
2	Capable Stan	VV	0 01 20	0 02 30	1 10	Composer	Johan Janey	Johnson		ASCAP	75.00%
						Composer	Adam William	Scott		BMI	25.00%
						Publisher			Pinicle Pint Publishing	ASCAP	75.00%
						Publisher			Zaney Publishing Co.	BMI	25.00%
3	My Mom	VI	0 05 20	0 06 15	0 55	Composer	Mark Anthony	Carter		BMI	50.00%
						Composer	William Jacob	Holly		BMI	50.00%
						Publisher			Zipzap Make it Hap Pub	BMI	50.00%
						Publisher			Winston Songs LLC	BMI	50.00%
4	Some Rap Beat	VI	0 15 03	0 15 50	0 47	Composer	Mark Anthony	Carter		BMI	60.00%
						Composer	William Jacob	Holly		BMI	40.00%
						Publisher			Zipzap Make it Hap Pub	BMI	60.00%
						Publisher			Winston Songs LLC	BMI	40.00%
5	Some Rap Beat	ET	0 17 30	0 18 10	0 40	Composer	Johan Janey	Johnson		ASCAP	100.00%
						Publisher			Pinicle Pint Publishing	ASCAP	100.00%
6	Lame Logo Stinger Boing 187	Logo	0 18 10	0 18 15	0 05	Composer	Julie Anne	Conway		BMI	100.00%
						Publisher			Pinicle Pint Publishing	ASCAP	100.00%

COPYRIGHT AND OWNERSHIP
Breaking the Myths
Ownership is everything.

***I'm not a lawyer, but I have a good understanding of how this works. If you are confused, do not take this as legal advice. You can chat with me for clarity or ask a lawyer.

Let's go with Q&A style for this section. This is the **extremely** simple version of the conversation I have with a lot of my students regarding copyright and how it works.

Question: Do I need to copyright my work with the US Copyright Office a copyright?

Answer: No you do not.You do not copyright your music with the Copyright Office, you register it.

Question: Why?

Answer: Because copyright in the United States is a right of ownership upon creation. Meaning, when you create something in a tangible form, you own the copyright to it. Copyright means right of copy. You own the right to determine if and how your creation gets duplicated. This term was invented WAY before we had anything digital, so this could be seen as sheet music back in the day. Publishing your work professionally is also a way to make sure you are in good legal standing on your original work.

Question: So why does the Copyright Office in the US exist?

Answer: Not all songs written are published somewhere physically or online and can be difficult to prove that someone is the rightful owner in court. For example, if you write music but do not consider yourself an artist or want to shop your music to other artists, you are wise to register your music with the copyright office because it creates a legal paper trail and very difficult for someone to successfully steal your song outright. Once you send your beloved song out to the internet, you do not know exactly where it will end up.

Question: My song is published online. Do I still have to register with the US Copyright Office?

Answer: You don't have to, but it's a good idea.

Question: If I have a lot of songs to copyright with the office, won't it cost a lot of money?

Answer: No, you can submit a body of work as a collection and copyright multiple songs at the same time as one file. Think of your songs as a chapter in a book, you wouldn't submit your book to register the copyright chapter by chapter, would you? That would be insane and paranoid.

Question: Whats the benefit of registering?

Answer: If you sue someone of using your song in court, the lawyer will have an easier time proving your case and may even be able to sue for damages and anything owed to you, but a sloppy job on proving your ownership could result in you only getting credit for the song and not damages. Ask a lawyer.

My advice as a fellow musician - Register your copyright in a collection and do not let money or time be an excuse. Better safe than sorry. Its only $50. Most importantly, never say to me "I am saving up money to register my copyright before I release my music". Start back over at the top of the page and read this over page and over until you get it. You missed the assignment. You can always reach out to me and ask if you need extra help by going to http://musicadvice.io

COPYRIGHT AND OWNERSHIP
The Song and the Master
Ownership is everything.

**I'm not a lawyer, but I have a good understanding of how this works. If you are confused, do not take this as legal advice. You can chat with me for clarity.

The modern track can be broken up into two ownership types. The song and the recording. You may own the song, but not the recording. You may own part of the recording but maybe not the song at all. Let's break this down. Let's start with an indie artist who writes and records everything on their own. We will assume that the artist has their own publishing company and record label.

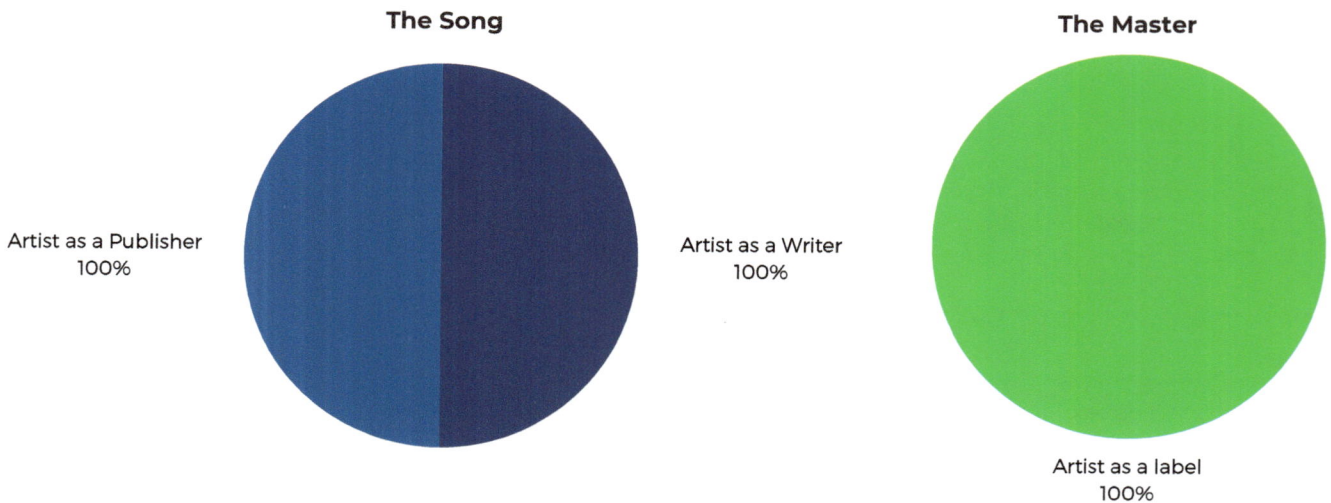

The Song

Artist as a Publisher
100%

Artist as a Writer
100%

The Master

Artist as a label
100%

"Wait, why does the "song" equal 200%? What is the matter with you? Did you fail math?"

No, I am pretty good at math. The song is confusing to beginners. It's done this way because a LOT of songs will have multiple owners. That means that the song may also have multiple publishers. You could have 4 writers, and two publishers and the writers may have different deals with their publishers.

Now, let's do an example where there is a band who has a co-publishing deal, worked with a producer and has a record deal. Let's get complicated!

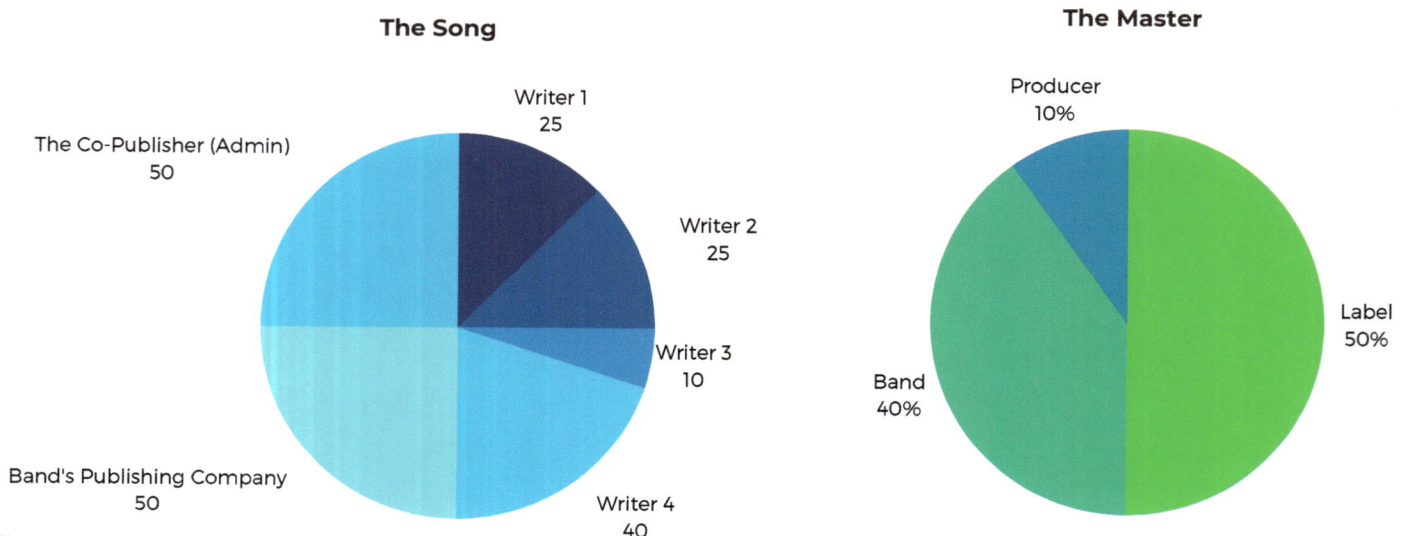

The Song

Writer 1
25

Writer 2
25

Writer 3
10

Writer 4
40

Band's Publishing Company
50

The Co-Publisher (Admin)
50

The Master

Producer
10%

Label
50%

Band
40%

INCOME SOURCES FOR ARTISTS AND SONGWRITERS
Where does your money come from?
Follow the money.

Touring/Live Shows – getting paid to perform live is a great way to earn income, especially on weekends or during a music festival. You can find booking agents or booking services to help you find gigs. You will usually get either a cut from the door, a flat fee, or a cut from the bar. Some venues will take a cut from merch, some will not. All venues are different, but it's best to schedule your shows well in advance and trade opportunities with other acts.
Merch – Selling merch to your fans is a great way to make income. You can get access to some great print on demand options by visiting http://musicadvice.io for a link to Printful. Easy print on demand.

Music Publishing – When you write music and license your music out for other artists to record, you are owed income from that deal. There "currently" a statutory rate of 9.1 cents per song on each song sold digitally or physically. This is not the rate for streaming revenue.
Sync License Deals – When your music is being requested to use in a visual project, there should be a fee given to you, whoever owns the master recording, and your publisher. Use Disco by going to http://musicadvice.io and registering for their software to send your catalog to these opportunities.

Brand Partnerships and Sponsorships – This is a business deal that can equate anywhere from discounted gear or free gear all the way to product placement ads on your content that pay thousands of dollars. There are way too many types to list them all. The new brand partnership model "typically" is through affiliate links online, paid review spots on YouTube channels, or gear sponsorships.

Streaming Royalties – These are royalties collected through earning income every time your music gets streamed on streaming platforms. Every platform pays differently, but the best way to get your music out online is to use Distrokid and getting a discount on your first year on http://musicadvice.io

Physical Music Sales – Your fans may still want something cool and unique from you. Things like vinyl records and cassette tapes have made a comeback in recent years. You're way more likely to sell vinyl than a CD now days. It's a cool factor. Getting something limited or special from your favorite local band or singer-songwriter as a fan is special. Make your fan feel more special by signing the product with a sharpie. You can build your products online and sell on your online store through Bandzoogle, which you can get started by going to http://musicadvice.io

Subscription Services – These are platforms that allow you to give your fans exclusive content online by joining a digital fan club. You can offer them all kinds of extra cool stuff. An example would be if you make beats, create a $5 a month subscription service where you get 10 non-exclusive beats a month. You can create these platforms on sites like Patreon or create your own through your Bandzoogle. Want to create your own or maybe even subscribe to mine? You guessed it, check out http://musicadvice.io

Live Streams – Live streaming platforms like Twitch, Facebook, YouTube and even TikTok are great ways to connect with your fanbase and earn tips from those who appreciate your live content. This can be live shows, or it can even be just you hanging out with your fanbase. Check out my Twitch page and ask me questions about your music career at http://musicadvice.io

INCOME SOURCES FOR ARTISTS AND SONGWRITERS
Where does your money come from?
Keep it going.

Crowdfunding – This is a great way for you to reach out to fans and offer them a product or service in exchange for giving your next project financial funding. For example, if you need $500 to get your album mixed and mastered, you can offer pre-sale discount for your album to help raise money. Instead of buying the album for $10 you can collect donations for $5 and send your fans who contributed to your campaign a digital copy plus an exclusive acoustic version of one of your songs. You can create your own crowdfunding platform on Bandzoogle by going to http://musicadvice.io

Public Performance Royalties (PRO) – Every time your song gets broadcasted to the public, your performance rights organization such as ASCAP or BMI will collect income for you based on the estimated audience. This can be anywhere from a bar juke box, a small venue where an audience covers your song, a TV show, Movie, all the way to a Superbowl commercial and everywhere in-between. This income goes to the songwriter and publisher, not the owner of the sound recording.
Non-interactive Digital Royalties (SoundExchange) – When your song gets played on digital radio stations, you are owed money from your sound being broadcasted to an audience. This income gets distributed to the owner of the sound recording, not the songwriter's and publisher.

Mechanical Royalties – These are royalties from digital and physical sales from distribution. This can be anywhere from your music being sold digitally on Amazon through your CD or vinyl record being in a physical record store, hipster stores (Urban Outfitters), or big box retailers like Target.

Video Monetization – When you get to a certain level of content and fanbase, your online video content can be monetized through companies placing ads on your videos. Many YouTubers get some or most of their income this way.

Music Grants – Depending on your country and your music, you may qualify for government funded art grants which uses programs to preserve historical or cultural music. An easy example would be a project that would capture indigenous drum music from American tribes or projects that are closely related to public music education like orchestras, opera, or jazz. There are hundreds of programs. These are difficult to get and take months to process, but you never know until you try. Some examples of grants would be New Music USA grants, Foundation for Contemporary Arts, The Alice M. Ditson Fund, New York Foundation for the Arts, Mid Atlantic Arts Foundation, Tennessee Arts Commission, and the COLA Individual Artist Fellowship.

Session Work – If you sing or play an instrument, you can get paid to perform on other people's music. You can start with friends or other local acts and work your way up to connecting with studios and producers in your area or online. You will either be paid as work for hire (no ownership) or you would be paid a percentage of the master recording. This means that you would earn some income from music sales and streams. Some deals can be a mix of both. I recommend distributing through Distrokid, so that you can pay out others on your project as well as getting paid yourself. Check out http://musicadvice.io for that discount on membership.

Teaching – now days people can have tutors for everything including songwriting. If you are at least at some sort of mid-level skillset on your craft and have patience, teaching may be a good option for you. There are many teachers who are making a killing teaching their craft to others. If you have 10 students and you are charging $50 per hour lesson (which is low), that is 10 hours of work a week and bring you in an extra $2,000 per month. Now build that up to 30 students and you are at a solid $72,000 a year on just part time income. That should be enough to free you up to do music full time while having time for gigs, family and promoting your music.

INCOME SOURCES FOR ARTISTS AND SONGWRITERS
Where does your money come from?
Let's go down the rabbit hole.

NFTs – Right now at the time of writing this book, people will either roll their eyes, be confused or get really excited about this NFTs. They are new to the public conversation and a lot of people who aren't internet savvy do not understand them, yet. But I think that since NFTs have been around for a few years and still gaining traction, that it's safe to say to you, "get over it, NFTs are here to stay." My very simple explanation to you of an NFT is a digital item that can be created and serialized much like a physical item in limited quantity.

This creates value by simple supply and demand. If you are giving your music away for free, it has a value in the marketplace at zero dollars. If you make 50 exclusive files of the same song, and sell them to the public, they are valued at whatever the market pays for them. The great thing about NFTs is that as the creator, you get to decide how many you make and how much "commission" you get if it gets resold again.

Let's say you sell me an NFT for $100 of an exclusive song that I can only hear if I own the NFT, and you mandate that you get a 10% cut of the sale if I sell that song to my friend to enjoy. I turn around and sell the song for $150. You get $15 and I keep $135. This keeps happening in succession, and the value of it goes up and down, but you will always get 10% of the transaction. Think of it like a baseball card, except the person on the card holding the bat gets a cut from the sale every time its sold on eBay. If you want to go down the rabbit hole with me on NFTs you can join me by hanging out with me on http://musicadvice.io by live stream, videos, or podcasts where you can ask me questions. Of course, my music club subscribers get priority.

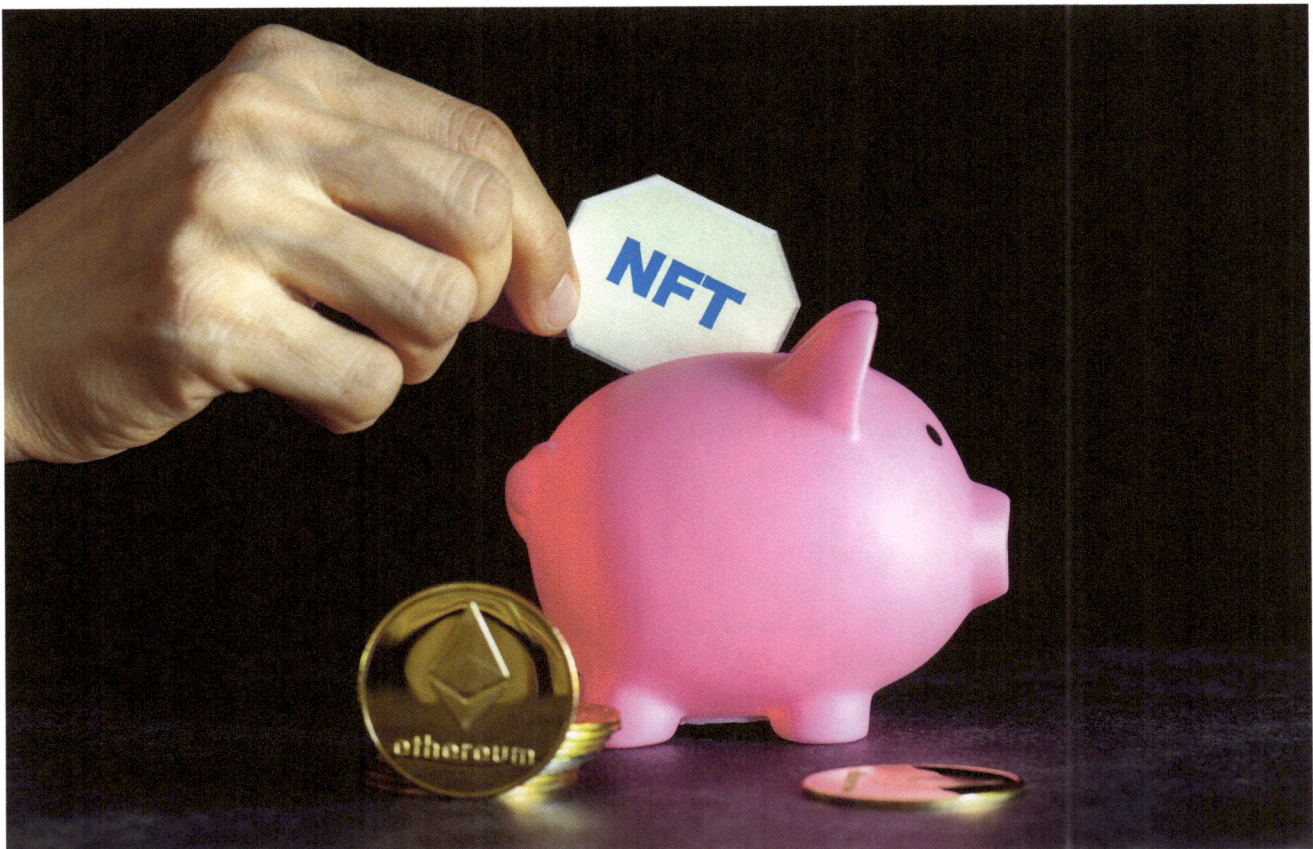

WHO'S WHO IN THE INDUSTRY
The people and institutions that you need to know
...and what they can do for you.

ORGANIZATIONS OR COMPANIES THAT PAY YOU

PRO (Performing Rights Organization) – These are organizations that monitor your song's 'public performance royalties'. You would need to register yourself with one of these organizations as a songwriter. Your song can ONLY be in one of these. You would need to register your account as a songwriter as well as a publisher on ASCAP. It's important to have both. There is a fee for this, but you are leaving money on the table if you do not and will not be able to completely register a song. Every song will need a publishing entity assigned. With BMI you can have a free writer account and still register your music without a publisher, it will just default you as the publisher. These organizations work specifically with songwriters and their rights. They monitor the song's intellectual properties, not the recording.

Your royalties can come from film, television, gaming, bars, clubs, juke boxes, commercials, department stores, dining venues, and anywhere else that your song is broadcasted to the public. If you aren't registering every song with a PRO, you are leaving money on the table. Also, pet peeve... Don't say you are "signed" to ASCAP, BMI, or SESAC... anyone can join with a small fee... and they are NOT publishing companies. Everyone in the industry will think you're a joke. Just say, "I'm an ASCAP writer", or "My publishing company uses BMI", etc. Be a pro. The most important thing you will need is to your "IPI number" as this is the number that people will need to pay you. Put your membership and your IPI number in your Meta-data. Make their life easy.

THE 3 PROS IN THE UNITED STATES

ASCAP (American Society of Composers, Authors, and Publishers)
www.ascap.com
Cost
Writer - $50
Publisher - $50
Writer and Publisher - $100

BMI (Broadcast Music, Inc.)
www.bmi.com
Cost
Writer – Free
Publisher - $150 to $250

SESAC (Society of European Stage Authors and Composers)
www.sesac.com
Invite Only

MORE ORGANIZATIONS YOU WILL NEED

Sound Exchange – A nonprofit rights collection management institution, and the only organization designated by the US Congress to collect and pay out digital performance royalties for non-interactive sound recordings. They pay featured and non-featured artists on non-interactive digital sound recordings, such as satellite radio, commercial webcasts like cable or satellite music listening channels, and most digital services where a listener cannot choose what song is played. Joining Sound Exchange is free. You should join ASCSAP, BMI, or SESAC as well as Sound Exchange as they handle a different type of royalty and deal with recordings rather than song rights.

WHO'S WHO IN THE INDUSTRY

The people and institutions that you need to know
...and what they can do for you.

MLC (Mechanical License Collective) - a nonprofit organization designated by the U.S. Copyright Office pursuant to the historic Music Modernization Act of 2018. The MLC began administering blanket mechanical licenses to eligible streaming and download services (digital service providers or DSPs) in the United States. The MLC will then collect the royalties due under those licenses from the DSPs and pay songwriters, composers, lyricists, and music publishers. You should join ASCSAP, BMI, or SESAC and Sound Exchange as well as the MLC as they handle a different type of royalty and deal with songwriters' royalties from streaming services.

Digital Distribution Companies – A for profit service that will collect your records, help you organize your rights, and put your music on digital platforms. These companies collect mechanical (or sales) royalties for labels and artists. You will need a distributor to get your music on platforms like Pandora, Spotify, YouTube Music, Apple Music, Tidal, etc. The distribution platform which is fully endorsed by Blake Makes Music is Distrokid. I use Distrokid because it allows me to pay collaborators, it's always on the cutting edge, inexpensive, has the most stores that they release your music in, and won't take any percentage of your royalties.

You can **learn more** and get a first-year discount by going to http://musicadvice.io/

Patreon – a service that allows you to create a digital fan club for your close-knit fans of your music or other art. You can create or release specific content to subscribers or create other types of benefits for them to help create special experiences for your most dedicated of fans. You can set up a per release, per month or per week paywall for your extra content. A lot of artists who know what they are doing when creating a community that they can monetize from, will often times make most of their income from their exclusive direct to fan content. For example, if you have 1,000 people giving you 5 bucks a month for a free non-exclusive beat a week, you can create a business on this model. If you want to see what others are doing on Patreon, come visit the podcast to help explain this business model for musicians. It's a game changer for a lot of creators.

If you want to subscribe to the Blake Makes Music Patreon you can check out http://musicadvice.io/

Music Publisher – companies that sign songwriters and their catalog of songs to solicit the music to artists, film, TV, video games, and more. Publishers will typically ask for all the publishers' share of your song, which equates to 50% of the income from the song itself (not the recording) Sync Fees and Public Performance Royalties. This is a standard deal. Some publishers will do what is called an admin deal, where they will take care of the paperwork for you and typically ask for 25% of your income from the song (half the publishing share) but are less likely to solicit your music. They just take care of the contracts. Most major labels have a publishing wing where the artists will connect to their neighboring publishing company to pair songwriters to artists. The publishing company is typically where the songs are created, usually in a team setting for an artist. If a film wants to use a song, they will need to get permission from both the publisher and record label as well as pay what is called a "Sync Fee" to the publisher, which you and the publisher will split 50/50.

Record Label – the owner of a song's recording. Traditionally, a record label will pay for an artist to record a song or album called an "advance", which is basically a loan. There is no interest attached to this loan, but large labels will typically dissect ownership to less than 20% and your advance will be paid before you collect anything. The record label is an old, antiquated model. Now days, you do not need one. You are the record label. You don't need a loan. That's dumb when everyone can do this on their own, so don't buy into the hype. I'd much rather you get 1,000 fans paying you $10 a month. That is much more achievable anyways, and 100% in your control. With a $36 a year on Distrokid, you can have your own record label. Boom.

WHO'S WHO IN THE INDUSTRY
The people and institutions that you need to know
...and what they can do for you.

Music Library – a type of publishing company that will sign a song rather than a songwriter. Then the library will publish a large database of music where the license is built into a quick transaction over self-service software or website. Most music placed in media these days are sourced from music libraries as they are quick, easy, and cheaper than dealing with traditional publishers. Libraries are also typically easier to get content in, as they work off a large selection made available to the music supervisor. The more music of quality that they must fit a specific situation, need or scene the more potential the music has of being selected. As a songwriter, your income will be split up exactly like a traditional music publisher (usually). Every library is different and some of them even specialize in genre or types of music. Most music in libraries would also categorize by film genres such as horror, sci-fi, suspense, romance as well as traditional music genres. The music is searched and found by extremely detailed meta-data such as BPM, feel, key, lyrics, mood, and more. This also replaces the need for someone looking to secure a license from having to get both a song and recording license, because the library takes care of the legal paperwork for both.

COMMON ROLES IN MUSIC CREATION
You can be any of these, or a combination of them depending on what you are doing on a project. Sometimes labels are important, and sometimes they are not. For example, an independent artist may do all of these on their own.

Commercial Music Producer – composers, producers or artists who make music specifically for film and television. They usually are putting music in a music library and arranged music in a specific format that is media friendly.

Composer – Someone who creates music specifically to picture that has already been shot. The process for a composer is much different than a typical producer or artist and requires a different set of musical skills to be successful.

Music Producer – Someone who creates or spearheads a creative project. Not all producers make beats and not all beat-makers are producers. Think of them like being the director of a movie. Sometimes a director of a movie will also be the screenwriter (songwriter). Some directors will also act in the film (artist), and some directors hold the camera and operate as a cinematographer (audio engineer). If you are running the project, you are a producer. Don't agree with me? Then explain to me what a metal music producer does. Where are the beats? Music producers can make income from the songwriting ownership, license, mechanical royalties, and song sales and/or a per project work for hire. All deals are negotiable with a producer.

Recording Artist – A musician who performs music on a recording. This usually is referring to a singer or a band. That was easy.

Songwriter(s) – The person or group who write lyrics, melody, and rhythm to contribute to a completed song or work of music.

Lyricist – A type of songwriter that does not write music or melody and only writes lyrics. Can also be considered a poet, but when working in a group songwriting session or may be the lead on lyrics. A good example of this type of songwriter is Bernie Taupin.

WHO'S WHO IN THE INDUSTRY
The people and institutions that you need to know
...and what they can do for you.

Top Liner – A songwriter who writes lyrics and melody over music that is already made or recorded. This is common with genres such as hip-hop and pop where sometimes the producer is detached from the 2nd half of the creative writing process by selling or licensing beats to an artist. A top-liner is still a songwriter but may not be proficient in an instrument or production enough to write and record their own songs, so the writing process for them is flipped or they may be in a writing group where vocal writing and arranging is their strong suit and someone else may be a more efficient producer or instrumentalist. It just describes their place in the songwriting production process.

Writing Camp – A group of songwriters, musicians and producers who collaborate on writing music with the purpose of shopping out a collective work to publishing companies in hopes of it being assigned to a major recording artist. Sometimes these are orchestrated by a publishing company, A&R reps, or freelance songwriters to write more efficiently for the marketplace.

Audio Engineer – an audio technician who typically works in a studio environment that oversees getting the audio quality be at its absolute best within a project's budget. Most of the time, engineers will report to the producers, artists, labels, and publishers. Some engineers will also help develop an artist to get the best out of their performance, therefor should also be considered a producer with credit on that project.

Tracking Engineer – One type of audio engineer that typically will focus their skills on recording the initial performance for the session while capturing the best takes from musicians and incoming audio quality from pre-amps, microphones and outboard gear.

Mixing Engineer – One type of audio engineer that typically works with the finished tracks, and will mix the tracks by using effects, volume, panning, automation and other mixing techniques to get the raw tracks to sound their best before being mastered.

Mastering Engineer - A kind of audio engineer that focuses on the very last stage of the production process. They will use EQ, compression and other tools to make sure that your mix translates into different mediums while sounding great. Another role of a mastering engineer is to make sure that if you are releasing an album, that the songs all sound as cohesive as possible with timing transitions, fades, and more as opposed to it sounding like a collection of singles that are compiled in a compilation.

Producing   **Tracking**   **Mixing**   **Mastering**

WHO'S WHO IN THE INDUSTRY
The people and institutions that you need to know
...and what they can do for you.

PEOPLE YOU SHOULD KNOW

A&R (Artist and Repertoire) – The individual or department within a publishing company or record label that is responsible for scouting talent, signing new talent to rosters, and managing the recording process for a release. They are also responsible for connecting artists, songwriters, and producers to one another. A&R is also responsible for managing the contract process between the company and the talent as well as acting as a liaison. A&R sometimes can take on roles of a producer and manager during the signing process or during the recording session. A&R reps sometimes will be paid off of the signing of an act, which comes from the advance of the talent. This can be in addition to regular pay from the company or in lieu of. These people are connectors, deal negotiators, and project managers.

A&R at a Publisher – These reps will work with songwriters to bring them on publisher's roster to write for and with artists typically attached to a sister label. These scouts will typically focus on acquiring songwriters who have large catalogs of recorded songs and demos as they would need to put these writers in sessions with others and need the writers to be efficient and able to work with others.

A&R at a Label - These reps will work with recording artists to bring them on a recording company roster and can sometimes collaborate with other reps from publishing companies to complete a project. These scouts will primarily focus signing talent that have proven to earn income in the marketplace on their own or building undeveloped artists based on market trends, but these deals are typically less favorable to the artists, as they have zero leverage in deal negotiations.

Artist Relations Specialists – These are a type of rep who are like A&R but will work with major or indie artists on behalf of companies like social media platforms, music instrument manufactures, events, non-profits, and other companies. They can partner with artists for product endorsements, company sponsorships, special events, cross promotional market campaigns, and other projects.

Industry Relations Specialists - These are a type of rep who are like artist relations specialists, but instead of working with artists they will work with entertainment companies but with an added responsibility of B2B (business to business) account management.

Artist Manager – Someone who oversees the career strategy and operations of a recording artist, producer, or composer. These people are also connectors and should have the ability to connect the talent to new paid opportunities via connections, taking over the administration work, and solicitation of a recording artist. These managers should be paid a percentage of the gross income that an artist earns while being contracted. Percentages can range anywhere between 10 – 25%, however major artist managers have successfully taken 50% as they may be a major reason why an artist has any major success at all.

Business Manager – A manager who works on the accounting, taxes, investments, and financial health of an artist. They can also manage rights ownership, contracts, licenses, and other business decisions. Business managers typically will be paid either by fee, salary, or a percentage of the artist's gross income.

WHO'S WHO IN THE INDUSTRY
The people and institutions that you need to know
...and what they can do for you.

Session Musician – a musician that will provide instrumentation or vocals on a recording project and will typically be paid a fee for their work. Some session musician contracts can also receive a part of the master recording ownership and none of the writer's share, especially if the producer, artist, or songwriter cannot pay the session musician a reasonable rate for their performance and time. Some session musicians will split the pay of a project between a fee paid and smaller part master recording ownership in an independent release.

Music Supervisor – The person hired by a film, TV, or commercial project to select music with the directors and producers for a visual project. They are also in charge of securing licenses for the song and the recording as well as negotiating the sync fees. Music supervisors will use extensive meta-data tools like https://disco.ac or use music libraries for smaller/less expensive music needs to help search through songs based on mood, genres, lyrics, ownership, and more. The biggest reason why a supervisor will deny a track from an independent submission is because the metadata is not correctly filled out with the correct ownership and contact information. Clean and accurate meta-data is important to be found. Supervisors are also more likely these days to secure music from music libraries unless a director is asking for a specific popular song.

Music Coordinator – the person who will typically work with a music supervisor and the media production company to ensure all the rights to a song are correct. They will also create and fill out the cue sheet and then submit it to the PRO.

Music Editor – the person who will piece together, arrange, and insert a song into a picture within the video editing software for the production process. They also use audio engineering skills to make sure that the music is appropriately mixed during the postproduction process to capture the scene correctly with the director. Therefore, having stems and instrumental versions of your songs are extremely important, because the Music Editor may need to mix or re-arrange your track to fit a scene in the right way. Sometimes music cues will be missed from oversight in the planning process or due to re-shoots and the music editor may create original music (like a composer) or source new songs from music libraries (like a music supervisor) to fill in those gaps.

Booking Agent – A person who will solicit live performing acts to venues and festivals while taking a cut (5-15%) from the fee that the venue or event production company that would be paid to the artist. These agents will typically require an electronic press kit for consideration. Some states will prevent artist managers from also being an artist's booking agent due to conflict for interests and double dipping in an artists' income since managers would be paid already from the gross income after paying the booking agent their cut of a performance.

Radio Promoter – A radio promoter will pitch your music to a large group of radio stations on your behalf. They will typically charge a fee for their services.

Playlist Promoter – like a radio promoter, a playlist promoter will pitch your music to a large group of streaming playlists. They will typically charge a fee for their services. You have to be very cautious of these, as many of them use bots to artificially pump streams up. Streaming services can find these fake streams very easily now days, which would result in a ban from that platform. As a rule of thumb, if anyone is promising a specific number of streams, they are most likely a bot farm and a scam. The best way to submit to playlists is to do it on your own, use legitimate services, or to submit to official playlists through a streaming services' "For Artists" app.

DEFINING YOUR WRITING PROCESS
What songwriting process works best for you?
Try new methods, explore your options, and build from your strengths.

For you to be the absolute songwriting beast that I know you are, you need to get a good understanding of your strengths and weaknesses as a creative person. You then can use that understanding of how your mind works and let it lead to your ability to create the most efficient songwriting process for yourself. Nothing is perfect and your mood and energy levels will change day to day but relying on your process in hard times can get you out of a creative funk.

Most songwriters will say that they do one of the following.

- Write lyrics first
- Write music first
- Write them both at the same time (instrumentalists can sometimes do this)

You want to figure out how you like to write music. Do you like to write lyrics or music first? Figure that out and lean in on your strengths. Don't try and become something that you are not, be the best version of yourself. That includes your songwriting process.

For someone who likes to write lyrics first, your process may look like this... "Write lyrics, write vocal melody, write the chord progression in your DAW, write the instrumental melody in your DAW. Record the demo vocals. File your demo and write another song."

What about if you write music and then the lyrics?

Your system could like this,

"Create and arrange a completed instrumental track in your DAW, create a vocal melody, write lyrics, record your demo of your vocals in the DAW, file your demo away, start a new song."

Don't ever feel like you are less of a songwriter if you need to inspire yourself with writing the music first and then fit lyrics on top of your instrumental tracks. Plenty of super successful songwriters do this. A lot of them. If you started your musical journey as a producer or by playing an instrument, I would bet that writing the music first is how you mostly write your songs.

To make you more productive and give you some ideas on coming up with your process, let's break songwriting into two stages.

The Core Stage

These are typical core components of a song. The most important elements of a song and should be worked on first. These components should always be present in your demo as well as your final product.

- The Hook
- Lyrics
- The Vocal Melody
- The Chord Progression
- The instrumental's melody
- A song's concepts or theme (love, break-up, politics, etc... what is the story?)

Use the **core components** of a song to map out your own writing process. What do you like to start off by writing first? Put them in order and GO!

DEFINING YOUR RECORDING PROCESS
What production process works best for you?
Try new methods, explore your options, and build from your strengths.

The Production Stage

These are typical secondary components of a song. The part that can be changed, therefore should come secondary in the writing process when fleshing out your ideas. These elements do not have to be part of your demo but would absolutely be a part of your final product. However, if you can, mapping these elements out on your demo can be extremely helpful. These are things that a producer would typically assist with or help create if working with one.

- Beat and Rhythm
- Genre and Style
- Arrangement
- Performance

Use these elements from the **production stage** to figure out what you like to start off with when you are planning your demo recording or master recording. There is no right answer on how to write a song, other than not writing songs at all. Find the way you like to work by trying new ways, do a quick self-analysis and write it down. Writing it down and putting your process in a place where you will see it every time you write, is extremely important. That way, when you get stuck, just look at your process to get re-focused on what comes next. After you establish your songwriting process, the next thing to do is to come up with a recording system between your demo record and your master recording.

Developing a recording process

Real quick before we move on, we need to establish the importance of a demo recording. Why do you even need one? Can't I just record the master right away? Yes, you can, but it may be costing you a solid performance on the master as well as slowing your process down. Let's talk about what the demo is and why it's important.

Master Recording – A final recorded song meant to be distributed and listened to by an audience. Your final product. The stuff you're going to put on Spotify, Apple Music, YouTube, Pandora.

Demo – A way for a songwriter to record their ideas down in a temporary form. This is good for when songwriters may need to share songs with other industry people such as publishing companies. Demos should not be poor in audio quality. In fact many demos sound as good as a master recording. The demo is extremely useful to the songwriter, as it has multiple purposes.

For songwriters, demos can also be useful for a writer to copyright a song with the US copyright office as well as a way for songwriters to remember how the skeleton of their song is written so that they may not forget the song. It's also a great way for songwriters to listen to them later with a critical ear so that they may plan their production when they record the master recording. It's also a way for writers to get creative feedback on a song when showing to peers or industry. Maybe when showing peers, you hear a few times that your intro is too long, or your second verse needs work. Make some notes and re-do it in the master recording process. Another cool thing that I have seen, is for songwriters to make their demos available to subscribers on their Patreon or other subscription service. That's a cool way for a super-fan to get to hear something unique and cool that most other average listeners will never get to hear.

Now what? You need songs, recorded songs, finished songs. Well, if you want to build up your song portfolio, you are going to want to stick to the "demo stacking" production method. This could be life changing if you aren't doing this already.

STACKING DEMOS
Getting the most out of your time
The secret sauce to your productivity

Demo Stacks – A collection of demo recordings, that have not yet have moved on to the master recording phase. Then recording the masters for the entire collection of demo songs all at one time in a sequence.

Demo Stacking

First, write and record a bunch of demos. The number of demos to have completed can be any amount. I would say, more than 2 though at a minimum. After you have your collection of demos done, you then begin the process of recording the collection of final masters from your demo stacks. This helps you stay in a "phase" mindset. It is hard focusing on the songwriting when you are focusing on your perfect performance. Some people even stack 52 demos to record them all and release one song a week. After you record the performances of all your master recordings, you can then move on to the advanced production of all your songs (adding layers, overdubs, effects, etc...) followed by mixing all your songs that you stacked back-to-back from a mixing template (so you keep the sonic footprint the same), then you can finally master all of them.

What does this look like? Let's say we want to release one song a week for an entire year. We would need 52 songs, obviously.

Step 1 - Write and demo (x52)

Step 2 – Record master (x52)

Step 3 – Advanced Production (x52)

Step 4 – Develop a mixing template (x52)

Step 5 – Mix songs from your template (x52)

Step 6 – Master your songs (x52)

Step 7 – Create a release schedule (x52)

Step 8 – Upload your tracks to Distrokid to be released weekly (x52)

Step 9 – Develop a weekly marketing plan (x52)

Step 10 – Execute your content marketing plan (x52)

Wow! That was a LOT of work!

But what does that method get you? Peace of mind once you are done followed by TIME to put effort into your marketing plan. Now you have an entire year to focus on creating things like music videos, developing a fan base, playing shows, live stream, vlog, market to publishing companies and music libraires. Time is the only thing not for sale in the world, so you need to use it sparingly.

WHAT TO DO WITH THE MONEY
Put your money in the right places
Earning income vs earning wealth.

***I'm not a financial advisor, but I have an understanding of how this works. If you are confused, do not take this as financial advice. You can chat with me for clarity or speak to a licensed professional. All invested income should be money understood that could be lost. Only invest money that you are okay with potentially losing.

Your money generated from making music should be put into something that can generate you some more money. Even if you scored a big $10,000 check from a sync deal, you should always live within your means. Money from anything other than a job where you have a salary or clock in and out from will always be inconsistent. However, that does not mean you cannot consistently make a good living. This rule applies to everyone, especially the ones who are making a lot of money, making music.

The way our money system works isn't the way you "most likely" taught in school. The dollar you earn and put into your bank account, means nothing. Let me say that again. The dollar you earn and put into your bank account, means nothing. I fully believe that fiat currency, is fake. The only value behind the US dollar is that the government says it's worth something. The minute the global economy decides otherwise, your dollar is useless. Instead of thinking in terms of cash for a job, think in terms of hours. Your money earned at a regular job that you then put into your bank account and savings account, slowly loses value every single day. This is because of inflation. It will take more money to buy the loaf of bread every year, meaning more of your labor will be needed to make that purchase every year. Yes, but what about raises? What raises? Your 1-3% annual increase for the same job will never match up to the 4% cost of living increase.

If you feel like you are becoming poorer at a regular job every year, it's because you are. Now what about the year 2021? Inflation went through the roof. Did you get a 10-15% raise to match inflation? Didn't think so. So never depend on your employer to match your wellbeing or lifestyle. They only care about their bottom line. So, if the US dollar becomes worth less, the more dollars that get printed, what do you do? You build wealth like the wealthy. Through assets. The rich can take a single dollar and make it turn into two. Not through magic, but because they understand and exploit the system. You don't.

I would much rather be wealthy than rich. Rich is temporary. Wealthy is generational income. You generate wealth through assets. Assets are things like property that hold, retain, increase or generate more value. There is a reason why you were never taught finance in high school. They didn't want you to know about it. The system is designed to keep the poor, poor. Otherwise, who is going to work the minimum wage, low skill jobs? You get yourself out of poverty from absorbing knowledge. You improve your lifestyle, from knowledge. So, after you pay your bills and cover your expenses, you should save some cash for emergencies. But if you have a bit of a surplus, even a little bit, it's my belief that you should invest it. No, I am not only talking about the stock market. First step to financial freedom, educate yourself. Knowledge is free. Its everywhere. Go watch some professional finance gurus on Youtube. Go google. Take a free class. The information is out there.

Let me give you some ideas on what you could invest that extra dollar in that you generated from your music.

1. Starting a music related business
2. Starting a non-music related business
3. Buying and selling stocks
4. Buying and selling cryptocurrencies
5. Buying and renting out real estate
6. Investing in yourself by taking online courses
7. Investing in a business
8. Buying in garage sales and selling on eBay
9. Buying better equipment to create better content
10. Advertising your content online to find more fans.

Your financial strategies should be extremely thought through. I chose real estate, businesses and crypto but you may decide to do something else. That is great too if you know what you are doing. I get my royalties paid out in crypto by linking my Distrokid account to an investment app that has a debit card and bank account number.If you want to do that to or want to ask me more about it, you already know ... http://musicadvice.io

Music Theory Cheat Sheet
Just the basics

The music theory rabbit hole goes deep, but you just need to know enough to get started. Here are some super basics.

Note Names

C D E F G A B

Lead-sheet symbols

C Dm Em F G Am B°

C: I ii iii IV V vi vii°

Roman numerals
(require key designation)

whole note

half notes (equal 1/2 of a whole note)

quarter notes (equal 1/4 of a whole note)

eighth notes (equal 1/8 of a whole note) (can be beamed or flagged)

sixteenth notes (equal 1/16 of a whole note) (can be beamed or flagged)

thirty-second (32nd) notes (equal 1/32 of a whole note) (can be beamed or flagged)

Rests

whole rest   half rest   quarter rest   eighth rest   sixteenth rest   32nd rest

Time Signatures

"How many?" 3
"Of what?" 1/2 notes (half notes)   4 1/4 notes (quarter notes)   5 1/8 notes (eighth notes)   6 1/16 notes (sixteenth notes)

Major Key Signatures

G D A E B F# C#

F Bb Eb Ab Db Gb Cb

Minor Key Signatures

a e b f# c# g# d# a#

a d g c f bb eb ab

For free and open source online music theory classes, visit www.MusicAdvice.io

GLOSSARY
Words and phrases that you need to know
Songwriting Terms

Bridge: Transitional passage connecting two sections of a composition. In pop music, typically after the 2nd Chorus, also known as the "C" section.

Chorus: The highlight of a musical piece in pop structured music, usually repeated at another point in the song. Also known as a "B" section.

Copyright: a legal right appointed to a creator (or assigned person) to musical material, that allows them to perform, record, publish, and control an original work.

Crescendo: a volume build-up in a music arrangement.

Decrescendo: volume decreases over time in a musical arrangement.

Dynamics: the volume differences between instrumentation, song sections, rhythms, or melodies in a song.

Genre: the classification of songs based on how they sound (rock, pop, punk, and rap are all genres).

Hook: the most important and singable part of a song. Can be vocal or instrumental.

Intro: The opening section of a song that is typically shorter and sets the tone of a musical work.

Key: The harmonic foundation of a piece of music. Will refer to the root-note from a scale that the song is based on.

Measure: A unit of measurement between two bars on a musical staff. Contains rhythmic and melodic phrases that contributes to a whole musical idea.

Melody: a collection of musical tones that contribute to a musical idea, phrase or song. Usually a melody is singable or hummable.

Meter: The feel of a song which is indicated by the number of beats in a measure and notated by the time-signature.

Modulation: key changing during a song.

Motif: an important melodic and rhythmic phrase.

Pre-Chorus: A section of a song that comes before the chorus that helps connect the musical ideas of the verse and chorus.

Publishing: An entity that represents a songwriter and solicits the song rights to opportunities. Publishers will also typically take care of administrative work on a song and contracts. The songwriter usually will have to sign over copyright to a publisher and register a song for the publisher to solicit the song accordingly. Some publishers will give a songwriter an advance, which is a loan given to a songwriter and is paid back by royalty earnings.

Tempo: a number indicated by beats per minute (BPM) that indicates the speed and pacing of a song.

Time Signature: In music notation, the compound number at the beginning of an arrangement and tells you the number of beats in a measure and the type of note that takes up one beat.

Verse: Also known as the "A" section, the section of a song that sets up the main "B" section.

Songwriting Prompts

Write a song about a big change that happened to you.
Write a song about a big event in your life.
Write a song about a chapter from a comic book.
Write a song about a complicated relationship.
Write a song about a conspiracy theory.
Write a song about a dog who has lost his way.
Write a song about a drunk night out.
Write a song about a famous person that you would like to meet.
Write a song about a fictional character that already exists.
Write a song about a fictional character that does not exist.
Write a song about a genre of music.
Write a song about a holiday.
Write a song about a part two of one of your older songs.
Write a song about a place you have never been.
Write a song about a politician.
Write a song about a social issue you care about.
Write a song about a strange kind of love.
Write a song about about yourself from the perspective of your parents.
Write a song about an average day.
Write a song about an instrument.
Write a song about arranged marriage.
Write a song about asking for help.
Write a song about being a parent.
Write a song about being afriad to breakup with someone.
Write a song about being Alone.
Write a song about being bullied.
Write a song about being confused during a breakup.
Write a song about being drunk at work or school.
Write a song about being dumb.
Write a song about being fake.
Write a song about being happy about a breakup.
Write a song about being homeless.
Write a song about being let down.
Write a song about being lost in a new place.
Write a song about being on a team.
Write a song about being poor.
Write a song about being president.
Write a song about being rich.
Write a song about being sad during a breakup.
Write a song about being the last surviving person left on earth.
Write a song about drinking alcohol in the morning and coffee at night.
Write a song about drugs.
Write a song about everything you did today.
Write a song about finding out something about your lover.
Write a song about floating away in space.
Write a song about forgiving someone.
Write a song about fossil fuels.
Write a song about health or being sick.
Write a song about hoarding possessions.
Write a song about how your great grandparents fell in love.
Write a song about insomnia.
Write a song about living forever.

Songwriting Prompts

Write a song about living on an island.
Write a song about living under a dictatorship.
Write a song about losing something like your car keys or wallet.
Write a song about love and hate.
Write a song about marriage.
Write a song about material posessions.
Write a song about meeting someone odd.
Write a song about money.
Write a song about not caring anymore about something.
Write a song about not wanting love.
Write a song about one of your favorite books.
Write a song about peace.
Write a song about people who are cruel.
Write a song about people's expectations of you.
Write a song about politics.
Write a song about revolution.
Write a song about running away.
Write a song about running.
Write a song about saying goodbye to yourself.
Write a song about siblings.
Write a song about sleep.
Write a song about social media.
Write a song about someone else's song.
Write a song about someone not respecting you.
Write a song about someone you can not live without.
Write a song about someone you lost.
Write a song about someone you love that doesn't love you back.
Write a song about someone you love.
Write a song about something no one knows about you.
Write a song about something that is in the news.
Write a song about something that worries you.
Write a song about something that you hate.
Write a song about something you know nothing about.
Write a song about sports.
Write a song about that introduces another person as an artist.
Write a song about that introduces the world to you as an artist.
Write a song about the current place you live.
Write a song about the desire to be sad.
Write a song about the last dream you had.
Write a song about the last photo you saw.
Write a song about the last thing that made you laugh.
Write a song about the last thing you learned.
Write a song about the last thing you watched on tv.
Write a song about the place where you used to live.
Write a song about the saddest story you have ever heard.
Write a song about the worst movie you have ever seen.
Write a song about thinking you are in love when you are not.
Write a song about trying not to cry.
Write a song about trying not to laugh.
Write a song about two enemies.
Write a song about two friends.
Write a song about wanting to get back together with your ex.
Write a song about war.

Songwriting Prompts

Write a song about what it would be like if you lost your memories.
Write a song about what it's like living on the moon.
Write a song about what you did not do yesterday.
Write a song about what you want out of life.
Write a song about what you want to do tomorrow.
Write a song about what you want to say to your ex.
Write a song about what you wish you had the courage to say.
Write a song about why people wear clothing.
Write a song about writing a song.
Write a song about your childhood.
Write a song about your ex wanting to get back together with you.
Write a song about your favorite food.
Write a song about your favorite movie.
Write a song about your favorite musician.
Write a song about your friend's lover.
Write a song about your hobby.
Write a song about your hopes and dreams.
Write a song about your idea of the perfect day.
Write a song about your imaginary friend.
Write a song about your last argument you had.
Write a song about your last day on earth.
Write a song about your last mistake you made.
Write a song about your life so far from being born to today.
Write a song about your regrets.
Write a song about your room.
Write a song about your senior year of high school.
Write a song about your sibling's or parent's favorite thing to do.
Write a song about youth.
Write a song that asks someone a question..
Write a song that has the phrase 'Don't hold back' in the hook.
Write a song that has the phrase 'help me' in the hook.
Write a song that has the phrase 'I don't remember' in the hook.
Write a song that has the phrase 'never saw it coming' in the hook.
Write a song that has the phrase 'something new is near' in the hook.
Write a song that has the phrase 'starting over' in the hook.
Write a song that has the phrase 'you can't quit' in the hook.
Write a song that has the phrase 'you were right' in the hook.
Write a song that has the word 'goodbye' in the hook..
Write a song that has the word 'happy' in the hook.
Write a song that has the word 'hello' in the hook..
Write a song that has the word 'sad' in the hook.
Write a song that makes people hate love.
Write a song that makes you feel happy.
Write a song that makes you laugh.
Write a song that makes you want to dance.
Write a song that motivates you.
Write a song that pushes you to be yourself.
Write a song that tells a story about an interesting person..
Write a song that tells a story about being disliked.
Write a song that tells a story about being misunderstood.
Write a song that tells a story about someone you know.
Write a song that that tells a story about someone you heard about in the news.

DEVELOPING A CONTENT STRATEGY & SCHEDULE
It's more than just about your music.
Try new methods, explore your options, and build from your strengths.

Let's continue with the 52-song example. Just writing, recording, and releasing music is not enough these days. No matter how good you are, there will always be someone better than you. However, instead of thinking of listeners of your music as fans... think of them as customers. Eww, cheesy. Yes, I know but it's true. You're the brand, and your songs are the products. That's at least cooler than selling socks. Here's the problem with being an artist, the noise. All the other music makers just like you are competing for attention online. "How do you keep someone's attention though? Its so intimidating!" Guess what though if you are selling socks there is just as much noise online. Don't worry because I am here to help you with that too! Let's go!

First thing you need to do is define your customer. If you listened to me earlier in the book, I told you to release your music on streaming platforms by using Distrokid. By this section of the book, I am going to assume that you have listened to me, and your first track is already out. I also hope that you have downloaded the Spotify for Artists app in your app store, created a personal Spotify account, and then connected the two of them. If you look at your demographics and analytics, what do you see? You may see gender, age or location. You may even have a couple of low activity playlists, too. What if your music didn't get any traction yet? That's okay! You can use your best guess in a minute. It just may not be extremely accurate yet.

You should use your own data to paint the picture of your most stereotypical listener. Let's say you make lo-fi hip-hop beats. Your demographics could be 18 – 25, male and you may have some activity in Europe and the United States. Let's call this made-up person, Mike.

For your "made-up" customer Mike, what other things are they into? They may be in college, have a unique hip-hop hipster look, and maybe they stream video games? They may have a chill personality, introspective, and trendy. What's in Mike's Netflix que? I bet Mike is smart or likes to think that he is. His sense of humor is nuanced and current. He probably studies philosophy or a social science in college. Only drinks fancy beer or mixed drinks and is into pop culture.

Most importantly, what OTHER artists does "Mike" listen to?

Figuring out what other bigger artists "Mike" likes is the most important part of this exercise. Write that down and come back to that later. We will need all this information towards the end of your content strategy.

After you define your customer, you should plan your content on where you believe that your most interactive listeners will spend their time online. For "Mike", let's assume that they like to spend their time online using TikTok, Instagram, YouTube, Podcasts and Twitch.

Now each one of these platforms act differently so you will have different content on each of them, most likely. Let's also assume you took my advice on demo stacking and you have some music scheduled way ahead of time. It's time to focus on the other type of content you are going to create that would engage with your potential audience. Let's break down content types based on your fictional customer we made earlier, Mike.

Based on "Mike's" information, he may consume content like...

Twitch – Live Music and Gaming (easy one)
YouTube – Hipster comedy sketches, left leaning comic-hosted political commentary shows, All Def Digital comedy, Mr. Beast, and trendy vlogs.
Instagram – Public figures that align with his political leanings, Twitch streamers, pop culture accounts, clothing companies like Levi's, H&M, and other artist accounts that have music like yours.
TikTok – Comedy sketches, gaming clips, random facts.
Podcasts – Pop culture review shows

DEVELOPING A CONTENT STRATEGY & SCHEDULE
It's more than just about your music.
Try new methods, explore your options, and build from your strengths.

Now, based on these potential types of content that "Mike" is consuming, we get to dive into the fun part.

1.What type of content will you be able to make that would grab "Mike's" attention?
2.What kinds of inexpensive ads can you buy online to put your content in front of more "Mikes"?

Making your content is important. It doesn't always have to be related to your music, but that helps. It's important to know your strengths and weaknesses in this phase, as you will need to make a lot of content, consistently. If you go outside of your comfort zone too much, you will burn out. The first thing you must do is start SLOW to avoid burnout but build up your content as you get better at it, just like you do with your music.

First question, what kinds of content can you do every week and not get tired of it?
You're going to need to release something, anything, every day. The more relatable your content is to your potential fans, the better off you will be.

Let's start with the easy one. Your music. Your music should already be scheduled right? Let's keep going with the example that you have 52 new releases coming out every Friday for a year. So obviously, every Friday you need to have something out online on all social media and content platforms about your release. Let's break that down. That could potentially look like this.

On release day

YouTube – A music video, lyric video or live performance of your song coming out, your TikTok as a reel.

Instagram – your album art as a photo, your TikTok as a reel. A story of you promoting your release with a thank you.

TikTok – a 1 minute preview reel of your track.

Twitch – A live stream of you playing your favorite game or chatting while you stream your music or a live performance of your new release.

You should use the same demo stacking method to produce content efficiently as well. Not all types of content will be able to fit into this model, but a few key types of media will. Everything listed above except for live streaming can be created in bulk and released later. This would also help you manage your time to do more productive work.

Now what about the other stuff?

Your devout customers will also be wanting content from you other than your music. What kind of stuff would you make? Let's base that from your ability, personality and your ideal customer, "Mike".

Again, making your content revolving around your music is a great idea, but not always a must. You can come up with a multi-use strategy. For this example, were going to make mostly music content, but some non-music related content as well. But anything that we make that is non-music related needs to be another outlet to connect with your "Mike".

Quick tip, TikTok can be a low effort, high viewer returns if you plan your content wisely. Instagram will take a little more effort but will allow you to connect with people more in depth, and finally YouTube is usually high effort content to produce but will allow you to create communities for your fans and reach new listeners. Plan your week accordingly.

DEVELOPING A CONTENT STRATEGY & SCHEDULE

It's more than just about your music.

Try new methods, explore your options, and build from your strengths.

Playlisting, email campaigns, press releases

So now there are a few other important things you need to do to keep this process up. You need to submit your music to playlists!

Here are the tools. They are all free!

Spotify for Artists - https://artists.spotify.com (Submit songs 2 weeks before release)
Amazon Music for Artists - https://artists.amazonmusic.com (Submit songs 2 weeks before release)
Apple Music for Artists - https://artists.apple.com (Submit songs 2 weeks before release)
Daily Playlists - https://dailyplaylists.com (Submit songs the Monday after release)

Submit your music to all these services every Monday! Music Monday, easy. Takes care of that! Now you need to take your contacts and send out a press release for your new music the day it comes out. You can send your press releases or email campaigns to radio stations, blogs, interview channels, influencers, podcasts, and playlists.

Anyone who can play your track to more people or give you an interview needs to be on this list until they tell you no. They will always have the right to unsubscribe from your email, but anyone putting out info and asking for music, should be okay with your submitting music to them for press or promo.

Use the service, **Disco** found on http://musicadvice.io to set up an email list where you can send playlists to your contacts.

Wow, that's a lot of work. Yes, it is! This is why so many artists never make it. They don't know how much work really goes into having a legit music career. Now that you know what is needed to go 100 mph, remember to start slow and build up your productivity. If you can't release 12 songs a year and back that up with promo and all the backend hard work, what makes you think you are able to do the same for 52 tracks? This goes back to goals. If you can't work fast enough to support your content, slow down! Start with a release commitment that you are comfortable with, so don't burn out. You will get there.

After you figure out your content, it's time to put it on a **calendar** and *stick to it*. Leave room for live performance, rest, admin work, your day job and family time.

An example of a weekly content schedule

MONDAY	Submit to playlists, radio stations, email campaigns
TUESDAY	Shoot a video for YouTube, TikTok video.
WEDNESDAY	Edit a video for YouTube, TikTok video.
THURSDAY	Release a video on YouTube, live stream on Twitch.
FRIDAY	Play a live show - heavy online promotion on new release.
SATURDAY	Play a live show
SUNDAY	Shoot extra social media content. (Photo, video, etc)

DEVELOPING A CONTENT STRATEGY & SCHEDULE
It's more than just about your music.
Try new methods, explore your options, and build from your strengths.

Other ideas for weekly social content

YouTube – music creation vlogs or interviews about your song that is being released that week. You can also release "*day in the life*" vlogs as these are very popular for fans too. Tutorial videos.

Instagram – two photo sets a week, copied TikTok to Reels and a new behind the scenes story daily about what you do musically, what you are working on or a good story.

TikTok – Quick music performances, replying, reacting, and duetting videos. Comedy sketches.

Podcast - Weekly interviews with other music people.

Obviously, there are more types of content and platforms. Don't only use these examples. Think outside the box, as social content should be something unique to you! This type of content is more difficult to stack up unless its mapped out extremely well. This part can be extremely difficult to maintain, but if executed properly you can really build a fanbase quickly. You are better off starting slow and finding your balance so that you can deliver the most content without burning out.

The best way to navigate potential social media burnout though is to pick one major platform and spend most of your efforts on that platform and the spread your content to other platforms.

Remember, your music and connections to fans come first before the extra content used to get your brand in front of more people.

If you go into extra social media content "guns blazing" and you get burnt out, remember my warning about starting slow. Always start with the music, the extra content is just the icing on the cake that can help capture your new fan and keep your current fans engaged with you. Its about building a community, not about getting more followers. There is a big difference. Crawl before you run. But the important part is to remain consistent.

An example of a weekly SOCIAL schedule

MONDAY	Upload YouTube Video, create TikTok video.
TUESDAY	Instagram live. Shoot Podcast Episode. Instagram Story.
WEDNESDAY	Instagram Story. Edit Podcast Episode and release.
THURSDAY	Instagram Story. TikTok video.
FRIDAY	Shoot YouTube Vlog
SATURDAY	Shoot YouTube Vlog
SUNDAY	Edit YouTube Vlog

THE CALENDAR FOR THE NON-PERFORMING SONGWRITER

Write, Write, Write, Demo, Demo, Demo, Protect, Protect, Protect, Shop, Shop, Shop, repeat

This model is great for those songwriters who just want to write songs and shop them out to other people. This schedule is based on how the publishing industry likes to receive music. Publishers will always ask for a COLLECTION of music that is being shopped to them because they need HIGHLY productive songwriters, just as much as talent. If you go this route, you need to eat, breathe, and sleep songwriting. Don't approach the industry unless you have at least 20 recorded demos ready to go.

When you shop your music to A&R reps at publishing companies, they want to get a collection of similar genre songs. Its good to pitch your music in a collection. You also can not release your music to streaming platforms, because the artists they are going to potentially pitch your songs to, don't want to be seen as doing a "cover" of an unknown artist.

Because of this, you also need to protect your music BIG TIME, as the second you send an email with your tracks to someone that is not released, you never know where it's going to end up. In order to not have your music stolen with ZERO recourse, you need to do the following.

Put your catalog of your demos on a PRIVATE playlist on SoundCloud. This gives you a date stamp, digitally. Then you register the copyrights in a collection on Copyright.gov afterwards, you can use Disco.AC to enter meta-data and pitch.

The Non-performing Songwriter - 15 songs a month.						
Sunday	**Monday**	**Tuesday**	**Wednesday**	**Thursday**	**Friday**	**Saturday**
Write an entire song	Record the Demo	Write an entire song	Record the Demo	Write an entire song	Record the Demo	Write an entire song
Record the Demo	Write an entire song	Record the Demo	Write an entire song	Record the Demo	Write an entire song	Record the Demo
Write an entire song	Record the Demo	Write an entire song	Record the Demo	Write an entire song	Record the Demo	Write an entire song
Record the Demo	Write an entire song	Record the Demo	Write an entire song	Record the Demo	Write an entire song	Record the Demo
Write an entire song	Record the Demo	Enter all Meta-data on Disco	Upload all to SoundCloud Private	Copyright entire collection Copyright.gov	Set up Contact List and Disco Playlists	**PITCH DAY**

Pitch Day - Email and pitch your music to Publisher A&R via Disco

THE SONG A MONTH PLAN
Write/Produce/Record/Release/Promote/Repeat

This model is great for those who need to do things "in the moment". This also works well for those who may have a consistent full time schedule working outside of the industry. To do all of these events, you only need to dedicated two hours of your time to accomplish each task.

Word of caution, this method is difficult to keep up with. Its very productive, but you need to prepare yourself for STRICT time management. You also will only get 12 times a year to promote your music. However, you are maybe a parent, work full-time, or both. You may need to work your life around the times you are free. This model works well for electronic artists, bands, and those who have a way to divert some responsibility and accountability to a partner.

On Sunday, Rest. You can also use this time to create low energy content such as photos for instagram, etc. Creating your social media content on one day and posting throughout the week is a big time saver for the rest of the week.

THE SONG A MONTH RELEASE PLAN

Sunday	Monday	Tuesday	Wednesday	Thursday	Friday	Saturday
REST CREATE SOCIAL	Write	Write	RECORD	RECORD	MIX AND MASTER	Complete Album Art
REST CREATE SOCIAL	Submit to Distrokid	PLAN YOUTUBE VIDEO	SHOOT YOUTUBE VIDEO	EDIT YOUTUBE VIDEO	UPLOAD YOUTUBE VIDEO	REGISTER PRO & SOUNDEXCH
REST CREATE SOCIAL	PUBLISH YOUTUBE VIDEO	Complete META DATA ie. Disco.ac	SUBMIT TO MUSIC LIBRARIES	Learn a New and Useful Skill	Learn a New and Useful Skill	Perform Live
REST CREATE SOCIAL	Submit to "FOR ARTISTS"	PLAN YOUTUBE VIDEO	SHOOT YOUTUBE VIDEO	EDIT YOUTUBE VIDEO	UPLOAD YOUTUBE VIDEO	Learn a New and Useful Skill
REST CREATE SOCIAL	PUBLISH YOUTUBE VIDEO	PUBLISH YOUTUBE VIDEO	EMAIL FANS DISTROKID HYPERFOLLOW LINK	Social HYPE	**Release Day**	Perform Live

Release Day — Submit to playlists via sites and email campaigns. Post on social, HEAVY.

THE SONG A WEEK PLAN

Write-Write-Write, Record-Record-Record, Release-Release-Release, Promote, Promote, Promote.

This model is great for those who like to work in stages and take their time on their music. This also works great for those who may have some free time, or go into a slow period at work or in life. Maybe your mind just needs to focus. This model is great because it allows you to create LOTS of content, but you won't see any benefit until WAY down the road.This process will take MONTHS of work and prep time, but it's effective!

Step 1 - Create

1. Write 52 songs and record each demo.
2. Full Produce and Record 52 songs.
3. Mix all 52 songs so they sound consistent.
4. Master all 52 songs so that they sound consistent.
5. Create 52 pieces of album art for each song.
6. Put all 52 songs in Disco.ac for meta-data and emailing promos
7. Set up your promotional email lists with all your contacts
8. Record 52 live performance videos (genre permitting)
9. Set up Distrokid for your 52 releases for the entire year.
10. Register your songs with ASCAP or BMI, SoundExchange.

Step 2 - Then Release and Promote

THE SINGLE EVERY WEEK FOR A YEAR PLAN

Sunday	Monday	Tuesday	Wednesday	Thursday	Friday	Saturday
Create and Schedule Social Media	Release to Patreon	Record YouTube Video	Edit and Publish YouTube Video	Release Live Performance	Release Day	Play Live Show
Create and Schedule Social Media	Release to Patreon	Record YouTube Video	Edit and Publish YouTube Video	Release Live Performance	Release Day	Play Live Show
Create and Schedule Social Media	Release to Patreon	Record YouTube Video	Edit and Publish YouTube Video	Release Live Performance	Release Day	Play Live Show
Create and Schedule Social Media	Release to Patreon	Record YouTube Video	Edit and Publish YouTube Video	Release Live Performance	Release Day	Play Live Show
Create and Schedule Social Media	Release to Patreon	Record YouTube Video	Edit and Publish YouTube Video	Release Live Performance	Release Day	Play Live Show

Release Day – Submit to playlists, radio, blogs, music libraries via sites and email campaigns. Post on social, HEAVY.

BEFORE YOU BEGIN
Let's build the foundation.
You need to establish a tiny ecosystem to collect fans.

Think of your music journey as starting a business. Before you offer a product, you're going to need a storefront or website to sell your goods. In music, the storefront is a little more complex but running your business as a music maker is WAY easier than opening up a restaurant, shoe store, or even a service business.

If i asked you what your favorite restaurant was, you would likely not tell me some fast food chain. You would probably tell me something unique to your location. Is it right to say that the business owner who has a small coffee shop down the street isn't paying their bills because they aren't Starbucks? No, that would be crazy. In this example, you are the small business. You are the local resteraunt, you are the small coffee shop, and no one has ever heard of you. Just because someone isn't famous, does not mean that they are not successful in music.

Don't think for one second that a small coffee shop owner held off on starting their business because they did not have any customers yet. That would be dumb. So you shouldn't either. Never make an excuse. Go. Make. Create.

You also need to know what it's like to fail before you can succeed. So these next steps will establish the foundation of your business, and also allow you to see how the new music eco-system works so that you can make mistakes on purpose, fail, and re-calibrate before you go hard.

First thing I need you to do is something kind of scary. I need you to write, record and release your first song. Put it out on all platforms, promote it, and submit to playlists, all to fail intentionally. Get the first song out of your way. Your first song will ALWAYS be your worst release. Your music quality should grow with your catalog of music. You have to get this out of the way. The only way to make great music is to make bad music first. You will always have taste that measures better than your skillset, get over it.

So here is the plan, jump...Then when you are swimming in the vast ocean alone, you will immediately understand that it's not so complicated. Don't wait to get good. If you can write and perform a song at all, you are ready. Open your business.

Having one fan is better than having zero, and the longer you wait to take the plunge, the harder it is to jump off that ledge. The good news is that If you can get one fan, you can get 1,000 fans. So use this "test release" to get ONE fan. Don't expect to blow up, that comes later. You're the little coffee shop down the street.

Later in the book you will see some schedules. Before you get to the schedules, you just got to aimlessly release music for the first time. It's not just about learning though. Setting up your content like your YouTube Channel, Spotify Artist Profile, and Twitch channel, takes time... Use this time to release ONE song, and on your own time finish out all the online locations you need to be so then it becomes a haven to shovel your content when you enter beast mode and you can focus on what you need to at the right time.

Cut this page, tape it to your wall

BEFORE YOU BEGIN
Let's build the foundation.
You need to establish a tiny ecosystem to collect fans.

You got your first recording? Amazing. Let's go!

You guessed it, another checklist.That makes it easy, productive, and effective.Make sure to check MusicAdvice.IO as some of these links are located there and offer discounts on these services or are free.

Before you release your first song

- [ ] Distrokid account - $35/year recommended to choose release dates.
- [ ] 10 Promo photos taken for your sites, EPK and socials
- [ ] Website created w/ domain name - Bandzoogle
- [ ] YouTube Channel - Live Performance, Related Content
- [ ] Twitch Channel - Live Performance and Chats
- [ ] Canva.com - Account for album art, etc. Free account is fine!
- [ ] Instagram - You need to get visual.
- [ ] Facebook - Yes, you need it for instagram business profiles.
- [ ] Spotify user account to make playlists
- [ ] Registered with ASCAP, BMI, or SESAC as both a songwriter and a publisher
- [ ] Registered with SoundExchange

- [ ] **Album Art Created on Canva.com 3000x3000 pixels**
- [ ] **Release date chosen. 4 - 6 weeks in advance.**
- [ ] **Song submitted to all streaming platforms via Distrokid.**
- [ ] **Song out on all streaming platforms via Distrokid.**

After you release your first song

- [ ] Disco.AC to pitch music, enter meta-data, organize demos and recordings.
- [ ] Spotify for Artists Account to pitch to playlist and see analytics.
- [ ] Amazon for Artists Account to pitch to playlist and see analytics.
- [ ] Apple Music for Artists Account to pitch to playlist and see analytics.
- [ ] Download a collection of music industry contacts - Playlists, Blogs, Radio, Supervisors.
- [ ] Create "print on demand merch, with Printful
- [ ] Create a mailing list on your website for fans
- [ ] Create a fan subscription service on Bandzoogle or Patreon

Setting Goals
Let's Accomplish Something

You know where the treasure is buried, so now let's draw the map on how to get you to it.

Print or rip out the page and stick it on your wall.

From

Date: _____

To

Date One Year from Now: _____

How many songs do you want to write?
- Per Day?   _____
- Per Week?   _____
- Per Month? _____
- Per Year?   _____

How many songs total did you write after one year?   _____

How many songs do you want to release?
- Per Week?   _____
- Per Month? _____
- Per Year?   _____

How many tracks total did you release after one year?   _____

How many YouTube subscribers do you have right now?   _____
How many do you have after one year?   _____

How many Instagram followers do you have right now?   _____
How many do you have after one year?   _____

How many monthly Spotify Listens do you have right now?   _____
How many do you have after one year?   _____

How many Twitch followers do you have right now?   _____
How many do you have after one year?   _____

How many TikTok followers do you have right now?   _____
How many do you have after one year?   _____

Identifying My Style

Who are you? What do you do?

You need to be able to explain your sound to others whether in person, online or in your branding.

Remember, branding is temporary and evolves over time. You can re-define yourself whenever you want or need to. Just remember that fans identify with your music, not your image. You need an image, but it can change easier than your sound.

Year: _____

I am a:
Circle at least one.

Songwriter   Artist   Producer   Engineer   **Composer**

I make what genre(s) of music?
Be specific."Everything" is a cop out answer.

My biggest musical influences are?
Name 3 to 5 artists, producers, composers, or songwriters.

_____

_____

My visual style could be explained how?
Use anything descriptive you can, you can also list other artists, eras, art, etc.

_____

_____

The person that is *most likely a fan of my music*
This part is difficult, but really helps you pinpoint who to talk to and who to market your music towards. No one on the planet is able to say "everyone" because even some people do not like The Beatles. Weird.I know.But don't waste your time trying to talk to people who don't want to listen.

Age: _____

Gender: _____

Culture or Counter Culture: _____

Favorite other artist(s): _____

Likes these brands: _____

Has these interests: _____

Uses these social media platforms: _____

Lives in suburb, city, or rural area? _____

Uses what platform to listen to music? _____

*Culture and Counter Culture examples:Skateboarding, Athletes, Musicians, LGBTQ, Hipster, Religions, Political Groups, Karens, Band Nerds, Middle-Aged Wine-o moms, Rockabilly scenes, Artsy people, Theater Kids, Blue Collar, etc...

A Publishing Split Sheet for Co-Songwriters
in 4 easy steps:

Step 1 – Fill out all the info about this specific song.

Song Title: _____

Date: _____

Recording Artist or Band: _____

Label: _____

Studio Name : _____

Studio Address: _____

Studio Phone Number: _____

Step 2 – Complete the following info about each and every songwriter that contributed to this specific song. Cross out any blank spaces.

This is to confirm that we, the sole writers of the composition listed above (the "Composition"), hereby agree between ourselves to the following writers' divisions:

Writer #1

First name: _____ Middle name: _____ Last name: _____

Address: _____

Phone: _____

Email: _____

Publishing Company: _____

% of Song Represented by Publishing Company: _____

Additional Publishing Company or Publishing Administrator: _____

% of Song Represented by Additional Publishing Company: _____

PRO Affiliation: **ASCAP**   **BMI**   **SESAC**   **SOCAN**   **PRS**   Other: _____

Writer Ownership %: _____

CAE/IPI Number (if applicable): _____

Writer Signature: _____

Writer #2

First name: _____ Middle name: _____ Last name: _____

Address: _____

Phone: _____

Email: _____

Publishing Company: _____

% of Song Represented by Publishing Company: _____

Additional Publishing Company or Publishing Administrator: _____

% of Song Represented by Additional Publishing Company: _____

PRO Affiliation: **ASCAP**   **BMI**   **SESAC**   **SOCAN**   **PRS**   Other: _____

Writer Ownership %: _____

CAE/IPI Number (if applicable): _____

Writer Signature: _____

Writer #3

First name:_____ Middle name:_____ Last name:_____

Address: _____

Phone: _____

Email: _____

Publishing Company: _____

% of Song Represented by Publishing Company: _____

Additional Publishing Company or Publishing Administrator: _____

% of Song Represented by Additional Publishing Company: _____

PRO Affiliation: **ASCAP**   **BMI**   **SESAC**   **SOCAN**   **PRS**   Other: _____

Writer Ownership %: _____

CAE/IPI Number (if applicable): _____

Writer Signature: _____

Writer #4

First name:_____ Middle name:_____ Last name:_____

Address: _____

Phone: _____

Email: _____

Publishing Company: _____

% of Song Represented by Publishing Company: _____

Additional Publishing Company or Publishing Administrator: _____

% of Song Represented by Additional Publishing Company: _____

PRO Affiliation: **ASCAP**   **BMI**   **SESAC**   **SOCAN**   **PRS**   Other: _____

Writer Ownership %: _____

CAE/IPI Number (if applicable): _____

Writer Signature: _____

☐ Check this box if there are additional writers. If so, attach a sheet listing Additional Writers that follows this exact same format and is signed by all other writers in the attachment.

The writers hereby warrant, represent and agree that there are no samples, interpolations, replays, or other third party copyrighted material (individually and collectively, "Sample(s)") contained in the Composition. If a Sample should become the subject of a copyright claim in connection with the Composition and the Sampled writer(s)/publisher(s) are to receive a copyright interest in and to the Composition and/or payment of monies attributable to the Composition, then we agree that our own shares in the copyright and/or monies attributable to the Composition shall not be reduced unless we are the individual party responsible for furnishing such Sample(s). This Agreement shall be governed by and construed under the laws of the State of _____ (Insert State).

Step 3 – Make a copy and give it to each writer that is signing this split sheet.

Step 4 – Enter this song into the PRO you are registered with as a songwriter and publisher. When distributing through Distrokid, enter all songwriters, and agreed upon recording splits.

A Publishing Split Sheet for Co-Songwriters
in 4 easy steps:

Step 1 – Fill out all the info about this specific song.

Song Title: _____

Date: _____

Recording Artist or Band: _____

Label: _____

Studio Name : _____

Studio Address: _____

Studio Phone Number: _____

Step 2 – Complete the following info about each and every songwriter that contributed to this specific song. Cross out any blank spaces.

This is to confirm that we, the sole writers of the composition listed above (the "Composition"), hereby agree between ourselves to the following writers' divisions:

Writer #1

First name:_____ Middle name:_____ Last name:_____

Address: _____

Phone: _____

Email: _____

Publishing Company: _____

% of Song Represented by Publishing Company: _____

Additional Publishing Company or Publishing Administrator: _____

% of Song Represented by Additional Publishing Company: _____

PRO Affiliation: **ASCAP**   **BMI**   **SESAC**   **SOCAN**   **PRS**   Other: _____

Writer Ownership %: _____

CAE/IPI Number (if applicable): _____

Writer Signature: _____

Writer #2

First name:_____ Middle name:_____ Last name:_____

Address: _____

Phone: _____

Email: _____

Publishing Company: _____

% of Song Represented by Publishing Company: _____

Additional Publishing Company or Publishing Administrator: _____

% of Song Represented by Additional Publishing Company: _____

PRO Affiliation: **ASCAP**   **BMI**   **SESAC**   **SOCAN**   **PRS**   Other: _____

Writer Ownership %: _____

CAE/IPI Number (if applicable): _____

Writer Signature: _____

Writer #3

First name:_____ Middle name:_____ Last name:_____

Address: _____

Phone: _____

Email: _____

Publishing Company: _____

% of Song Represented by Publishing Company: _____

Additional Publishing Company or Publishing Administrator: _____

% of Song Represented by Additional Publishing Company: _____

PRO Affiliation: **ASCAP**   **BMI**   **SESAC**   **SOCAN**   **PRS**   Other: _____

Writer Ownership %: _____

CAE/IPI Number (if applicable): _____

Writer Signature: _____

Writer #4

First name:_____ Middle name:_____ Last name:_____

Address: _____

Phone: _____

Email: _____

Publishing Company: _____

% of Song Represented by Publishing Company: _____

Additional Publishing Company or Publishing Administrator: _____

% of Song Represented by Additional Publishing Company: _____

PRO Affiliation: **ASCAP**   **BMI**   **SESAC**   **SOCAN**   **PRS**   Other: _____

Writer Ownership %: _____

CAE/IPI Number (if applicable): _____

Writer Signature: _____

☐ Check this box if there are additional writers. If so, attach a sheet listing Additional Writers that follows this exact same format and is signed by all other writers in the attachment.

The writers hereby warrant, represent and agree that there are no samples, interpolations, replays, or other third party copyrighted material (individually and collectively, "Sample(s)") contained in the Composition. If a Sample should become the subject of a copyright claim in connection with the Composition and the Sampled writer(s)/publisher(s) are to receive a copyright interest in and to the Composition and/or payment of monies attributable to the Composition, then we agree that our own shares in the copyright and/or monies attributable to the Composition shall not be reduced unless we are the individual party responsible for furnishing such Sample(s). This Agreement shall be governed by and construed under the laws of the State of _____ (Insert State).

Step 3 – Make a copy and give it to each writer that is signing this split sheet.

Step 4 – Enter this song into the PRO you are registered with as a songwriter and publisher. When distributing through Distrokid, enter all songwriters, and agreed upon recording splits.

A Publishing Split Sheet for Co-Songwriters
in 4 easy steps:

Step 1 – Fill out all the info about this specific song.

Song Title: _____

Date: _____

Recording Artist or Band: _____

Label: _____

Studio Name : _____

Studio Address: _____

Studio Phone Number: _____

Step 2 – Complete the following info about each and every songwriter that contributed to this specific song. Cross out any blank spaces.

This is to confirm that we, the sole writers of the composition listed above (the "Composition"), hereby agree between ourselves to the following writers' divisions:

Writer #1

First name:_____ Middle name:_____ Last name:_____

Address: _____

Phone: _____

Email: _____

Publishing Company: _____

% of Song Represented by Publishing Company: _____

Additional Publishing Company or Publishing Administrator: _____

% of Song Represented by Additional Publishing Company: _____

PRO Affiliation: **ASCAP**   **BMI**   **SESAC**   **SOCAN**   **PRS**   Other: _____

Writer Ownership %: _____

CAE/IPI Number (if applicable): _____

Writer Signature: _____

Writer #2

First name:_____ Middle name:_____ Last name:_____

Address: _____

Phone: _____

Email: _____

Publishing Company: _____

% of Song Represented by Publishing Company: _____

Additional Publishing Company or Publishing Administrator: _____

% of Song Represented by Additional Publishing Company: _____

PRO Affiliation: **ASCAP**   **BMI**   **SESAC**   **SOCAN**   **PRS**   Other: _____

Writer Ownership %: _____

CAE/IPI Number (if applicable): _____

Writer Signature: _____

Writer #3

First name:_____ Middle name:_____ Last name:_____

Address: _____

Phone: _____

Email: _____

Publishing Company: _____

% of Song Represented by Publishing Company: _____

Additional Publishing Company or Publishing Administrator: _____

% of Song Represented by Additional Publishing Company: _____

PRO Affiliation: **ASCAP**   **BMI**   **SESAC**   **SOCAN**   **PRS**   Other: _____

Writer Ownership %: _____

CAE/IPI Number (if applicable): _____

Writer Signature: _____

Writer #4

First name:_____ Middle name:_____ Last name:_____

Address: _____

Phone: _____

Email: _____

Publishing Company: _____

% of Song Represented by Publishing Company: _____

Additional Publishing Company or Publishing Administrator: _____

% of Song Represented by Additional Publishing Company: _____

PRO Affiliation: **ASCAP**   **BMI**   **SESAC**   **SOCAN**   **PRS**   Other: _____

Writer Ownership %: _____

CAE/IPI Number (if applicable): _____

Writer Signature: _____

☐ Check this box if there are additional writers. If so, attach a sheet listing Additional Writers
that follows this exact same format and is signed by all other writers in the attachment.

The writers hereby warrant, represent and agree that there are no samples, interpolations, replays, or other third party copyrighted material (individually and collectively, "Sample(s)") contained in the Composition. If a Sample should become the subject of a copyright claim in connection with the Composition and the Sampled writer(s)/publisher(s) are to receive a copyright interest in and to the Composition and/or payment of monies attributable to the Composition, then we agree that our own shares in the copyright and/or monies attributable to the Composition shall not be reduced unless we are the individual party responsible for furnishing such Sample(s). This Agreement shall be governed by and construed under the laws of the State of _____ (Insert State).

Step 3 – Make a copy and give it to each writer that is signing this split sheet.

Step 4 – Enter this song into the PRO you are registered with as a songwriter and publisher. When distributing through Distrokid, enter all songwriters, and agreed upon recording splits.

A Publishing Split Sheet for Co-Songwriters
in 4 easy steps:

Step 1 – Fill out all the info about this specific song.

Song Title: _____

Date: _____

Recording Artist or Band: _____

Label: _____

Studio Name : _____

Studio Address: _____

Studio Phone Number: _____

Step 2 – Complete the following info about each and every songwriter that contributed to this specific song. Cross out any blank spaces.

This is to confirm that we, the sole writers of the composition listed above (the "Composition"), hereby agree between ourselves to the following writers' divisions:

Writer #1

First name:_____ Middle name:_____ Last name:_____

Address: _____

Phone: _____

Email: _____

Publishing Company: _____

% of Song Represented by Publishing Company: _____

Additional Publishing Company or Publishing Administrator: _____

% of Song Represented by Additional Publishing Company: _____

PRO Affiliation: **ASCAP**   **BMI**   **SESAC**   **SOCAN**   **PRS**   Other: _____

Writer Ownership %: _____

CAE/IPI Number (if applicable): _____

Writer Signature: _____

Writer #2

First name:_____ Middle name:_____ Last name:_____

Address: _____

Phone: _____

Email: _____

Publishing Company: _____

% of Song Represented by Publishing Company: _____

Additional Publishing Company or Publishing Administrator: _____

% of Song Represented by Additional Publishing Company: _____

PRO Affiliation: **ASCAP**   **BMI**   **SESAC**   **SOCAN**   **PRS**   Other: _____

Writer Ownership %: _____

CAE/IPI Number (if applicable): _____

Writer Signature: _____

Writer #3

First name: _____ Middle name: _____ Last name: _____

Address: _____

Phone: _____

Email: _____

Publishing Company: _____

% of Song Represented by Publishing Company: _____

Additional Publishing Company or Publishing Administrator: _____

% of Song Represented by Additional Publishing Company: _____

PRO Affiliation: **ASCAP**   **BMI**   **SESAC**   **SOCAN**   **PRS**   Other: _____

Writer Ownership %: _____

CAE/IPI Number (if applicable): _____

Writer Signature: _____

Writer #4

First name: _____ Middle name: _____ Last name: _____

Address: _____

Phone: _____

Email: _____

Publishing Company: _____

% of Song Represented by Publishing Company: _____

Additional Publishing Company or Publishing Administrator: _____

% of Song Represented by Additional Publishing Company: _____

PRO Affiliation: **ASCAP**   **BMI**   **SESAC**   **SOCAN**   **PRS**   Other: _____

Writer Ownership %: _____

CAE/IPI Number (if applicable): _____

Writer Signature: _____

☐ Check this box if there are additional writers. If so, attach a sheet listing Additional Writers that follows this exact same format and is signed by all other writers in the attachment.

The writers hereby warrant, represent and agree that there are no samples, interpolations, replays, or other third party copyrighted material (individually and collectively, "Sample(s)") contained in the Composition. If a Sample should become the subject of a copyright claim in connection with the Composition and the Sampled writer(s)/publisher(s) are to receive a copyright interest in and to the Composition and/or payment of monies attributable to the Composition, then we agree that our own shares in the copyright and/or monies attributable to the Composition shall not be reduced unless we are the individual party responsible for furnishing such Sample(s). This Agreement shall be governed by and construed under the laws of the State of _____ (Insert State).

Step 3 – Make a copy and give it to each writer that is signing this split sheet.

Step 4 – Enter this song into the PRO you are registered with as a songwriter and publisher. When distributing through Distrokid, enter all songwriters, and agreed upon recording splits.

CREATE YOUR SCHEDULE

MONTH:_____

Sunday	Monday	Tuesday	Wednesday	Thursday	Friday	Saturday

CREATE YOUR SCHEDULE

MONTH: _____

Sunday	Monday	Tuesday	Wednesday	Thursday	Friday	Saturday

CREATE YOUR SCHEDULE

MONTH: _____

Sunday	Monday	Tuesday	Wednesday	Thursday	Friday	Saturday

www.MusicAdvice.io

WEEK #_____

Your weekly writing and producing schedule. Get some music done!

MONDAY

TUESDAY

WEDNESDAY

THURSDAY

FRIDAY

SATURDAY

SUNDAY

www.MusicAdvice.io

WEEK #_____

Your weekly writing and producing schedule. Get some music done!

MONDAY

TUESDAY

WEDNESDAY

THURSDAY

FRIDAY

SATURDAY

SUNDAY

www.MusicAdvice.io

WEEK #_____

Your weekly writing and producing schedule. Get some music done!

MONDAY

TUESDAY

WEDNESDAY

THURSDAY

FRIDAY

SATURDAY

SUNDAY

WEEK #_____

Your weekly writing and producing schedule. Get some music done!

MONDAY

TUESDAY

WEDNESDAY

THURSDAY

FRIDAY

SATURDAY

SUNDAY

YOUR CONTENT SCHEDULE
Use this page to fill in your content schedule

This page should include all content types. You get a few of these pages because your strategies should evolve and change over time. Rip out or print then stick on your wall.

Cut this page, tape it to your wall

MONDAY	TUESDAY	WEDNESDAY	THURSDAY	FRIDAY	SATURDAY	SUNDAY

YOUR CONTENT SCHEDULE

Use this page to fill in your content schedule

This page should include all content types. You get a few of these pages because your strategies should evolve and change over time. Rip out or print then stick on your wall.

Cut this page, tape it to your wall

MONDAY	TUESDAY	WEDNESDAY	THURSDAY	FRIDAY	SATURDAY	SUNDAY

Lyrics

Verse 1

A1

_____

_____

_____

_____

_____

_____

_____

Verse 2

A2

_____

_____

_____

_____

_____

_____

_____

Chorus

B

_____

_____

_____

_____

_____

_____

Bridge

C

_____

_____

_____

_____

_____

_____

_____

Inspiration

Mood

Checklist

- [ ] Song Written
- [ ] Pre-Production Complete
- [ ] Song recorded
- [ ] Song Mixed
- [ ] Song Mastered
- [ ] Album Art
- [ ] Copyright
- [ ] Meta-Data Complete
- [ ] Song Submitted to Distrokid
- [ ] Registered with PRO
- [ ] Recording Registered with SoundExchange
- [ ] Video Recorded
- [ ] Social Posts Scheduled
- [ ] Sent to fans
- [ ] Sent to Music Libraries
- [ ] Sent to Playlists

www.MusicAdvice.io

Rhythm and Melody

Verse

A

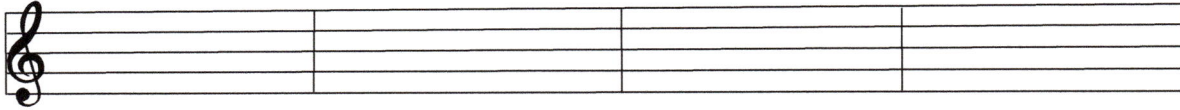

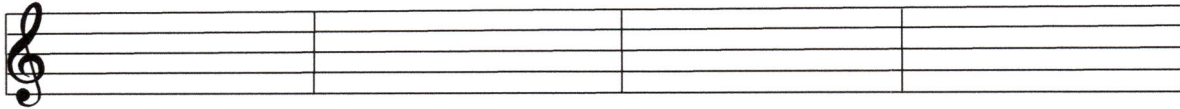

Chorus

B

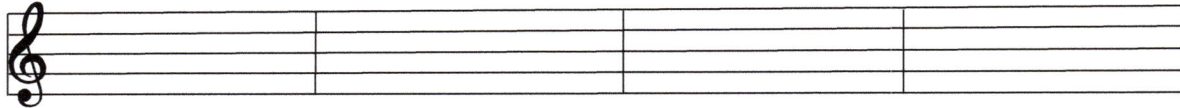

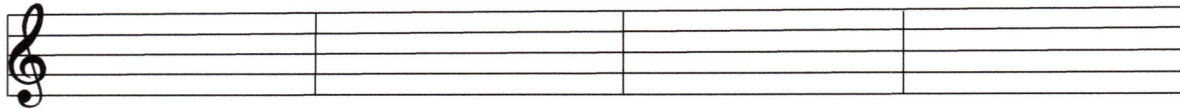

Bridge

C

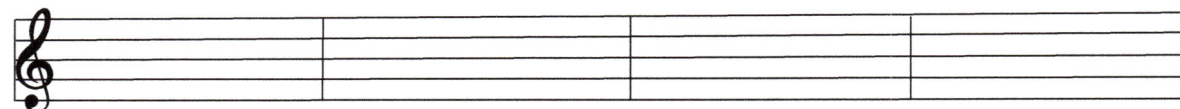

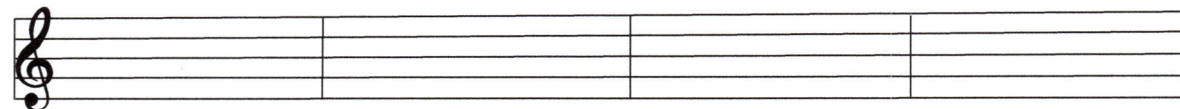

Chord Progressions

A

B

C

Song Structure

Lyrics

Verse 1

A1 _____

_____

_____

_____

_____

_____

_____

_____

Verse 2

A2 _____

_____

_____

_____

_____

_____

_____

Chorus

B _____

_____

_____

_____

_____

_____

_____

Bridge

C _____

_____

_____

_____

_____

_____

_____

Inspiration

Mood

Checklist

- [ ] Song Written
- [ ] Pre-Production Complete
- [ ] Song recorded
- [ ] Song Mixed
- [ ] Song Mastered
- [ ] Album Art
- [ ] Copyright
- [ ] Meta-Data Complete
- [ ] Song Submitted to Distrokid
- [ ] Registered with PRO
- [ ] Recording Registered with SoundExchange
- [ ] Video Recorded
- [ ] Social Posts Scheduled
- [ ] Sent to fans
- [ ] Sent to Music Libraries
- [ ] Sent to Playlists

Rhythm and Melody

Verse

A

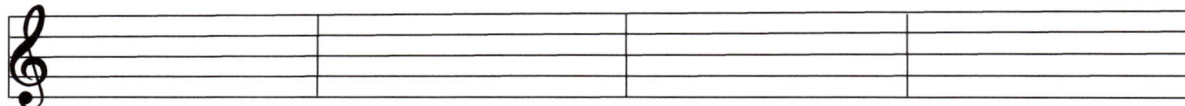

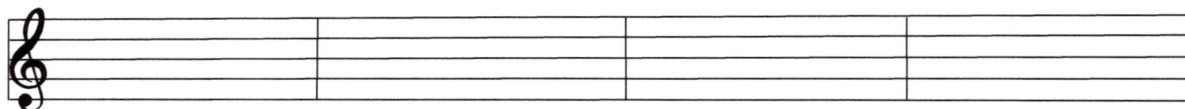

Chorus

B

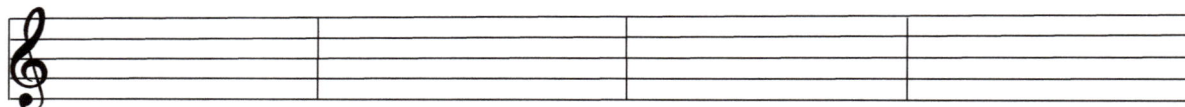

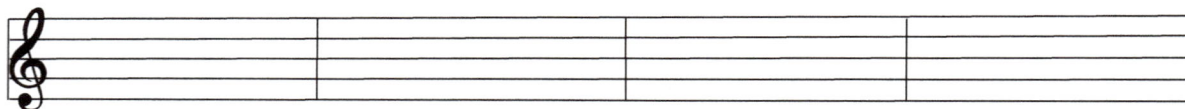

Bridge

C

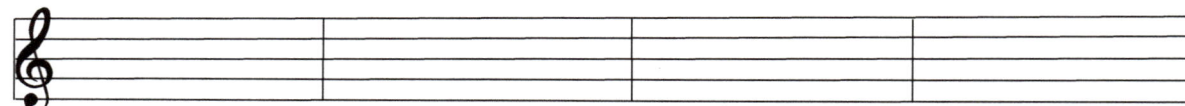

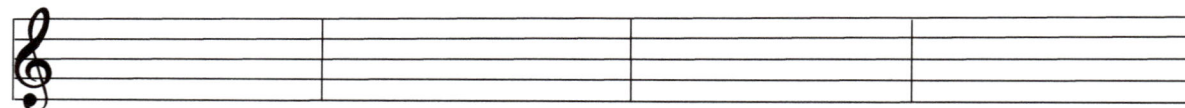

Chord Progressions

A

B

C

Song Structure

Lyrics

Verse 1

A1

_____
_____
_____
_____
_____
_____
_____
_____

Verse 2

A2

_____
_____
_____
_____
_____

Chorus

B

_____
_____
_____
_____
_____
_____

Bridge

C

_____
_____
_____
_____
_____
_____

Inspiration

Mood

Checklist

- ☐ Song Written
- ☐ Pre-Production Complete
- ☐ Song recorded
- ☐ Song Mixed
- ☐ Song Mastered
- ☐ Album Art
- ☐ Copyright
- ☐ Meta-Data Complete
- ☐ Song Submitted to Distrokid
- ☐ Registered with PRO
- ☐ Recording Registered with SoundExchange
- ☐ Video Recorded
- ☐ Social Posts Scheduled
- ☐ Sent to fans
- ☐ Sent to Music Libraries
- ☐ Sent to Playlists

Rhythm and Melody

Verse

A

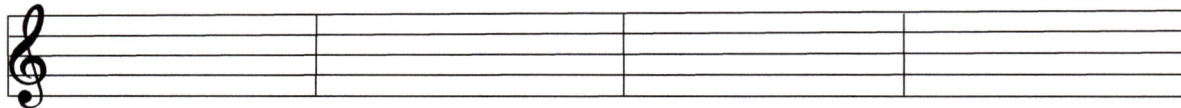

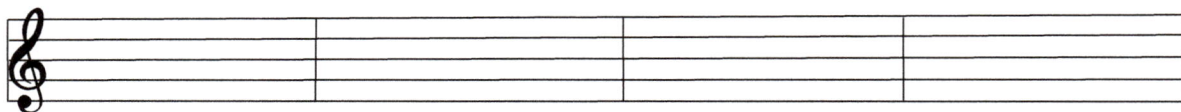

Chorus

B

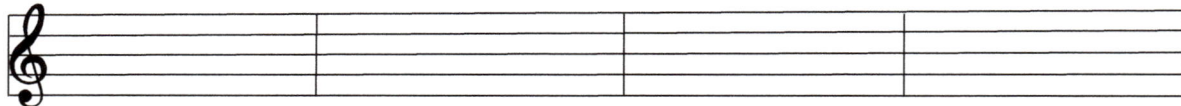

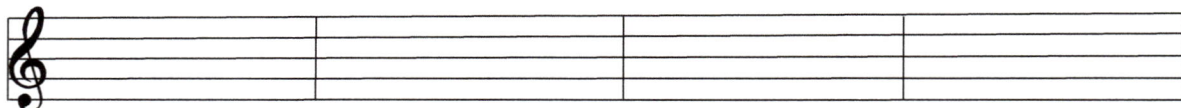

Bridge

C

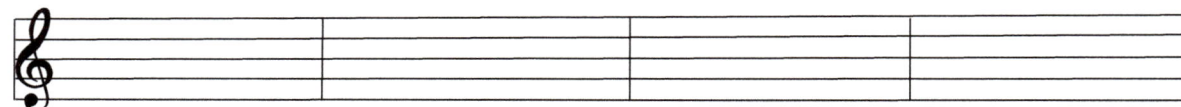

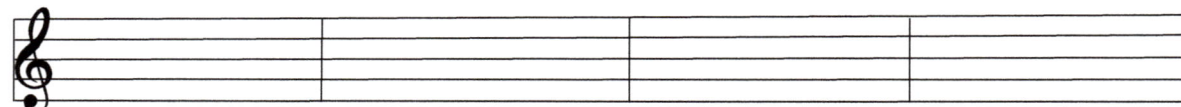

Chord Progressions

A

B

C

Song Structure

Lyrics

Verse 1

A1

_____
_____
_____
_____
_____
_____
_____

Verse 2

A2

_____
_____
_____
_____
_____
_____
_____

Chorus

B

_____
_____
_____
_____
_____
_____

Bridge

C

_____
_____
_____
_____
_____
_____
_____

Inspiration

Mood

Checklist

- [ ] Song Written
- [ ] Pre-Production Complete
- [ ] Song recorded
- [ ] Song Mixed
- [ ] Song Mastered
- [ ] Album Art
- [ ] Copyright
- [ ] Meta-Data Complete
- [ ] Song Submitted to Distrokid
- [ ] Registered with PRO
- [ ] Recording Registered with SoundExchange
- [ ] Video Recorded
- [ ] Social Posts Scheduled
- [ ] Sent to fans
- [ ] Sent to Music Libraries
- [ ] Sent to Playlists

www.MusicAdvice.io

Front

Rhythm and Melody

Verse

A

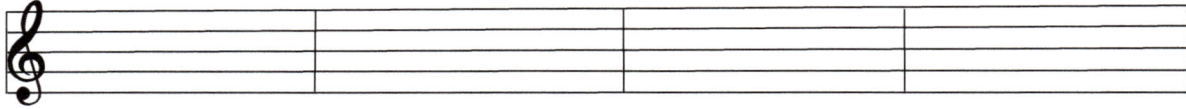

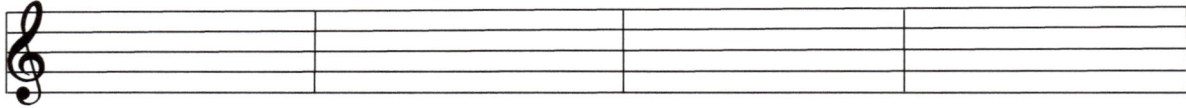

Chorus

B

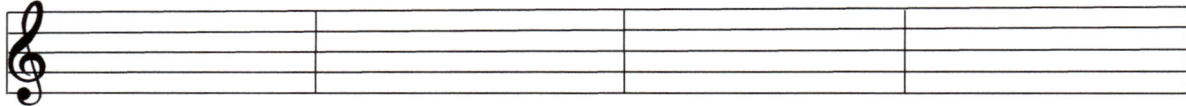

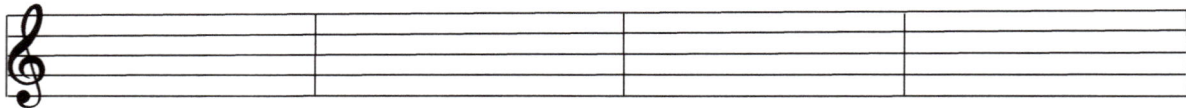

Bridge

C

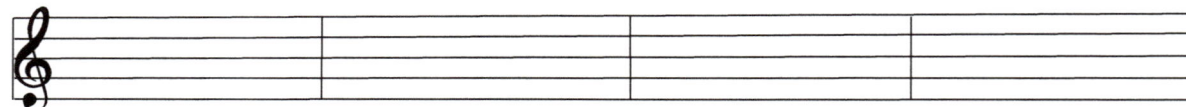

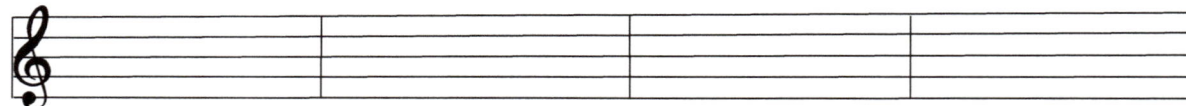

Chord Progressions

A

B

C

Song Structure

Lyrics

Verse 1
(A1) _____
_____
_____
_____
_____
_____

Verse 2
(A2) _____
_____
_____
_____
_____
_____

Chorus
(B) _____
_____
_____
_____
_____
_____

Bridge
(C) _____
_____
_____
_____
_____
_____

Inspiration

Mood

Checklist

- [ ] Song Written
- [ ] Pre-Production Complete
- [ ] Song recorded
- [ ] Song Mixed
- [ ] Song Mastered
- [ ] Album Art
- [ ] Copyright
- [ ] Meta-Data Complete
- [ ] Song Submitted to Distrokid
- [ ] Registered with PRO
- [ ] Recording Registered with SoundExchange
- [ ] Video Recorded
- [ ] Social Posts Scheduled
- [ ] Sent to fans
- [ ] Sent to Music Libraries
- [ ] Sent to Playlists

www.MusicAdvice.io

Rhythm and Melody

Verse

A

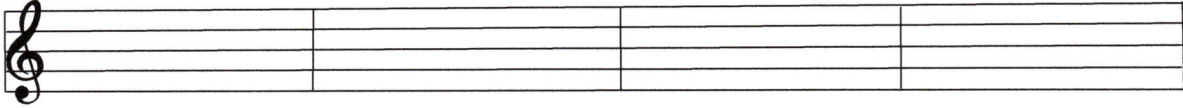

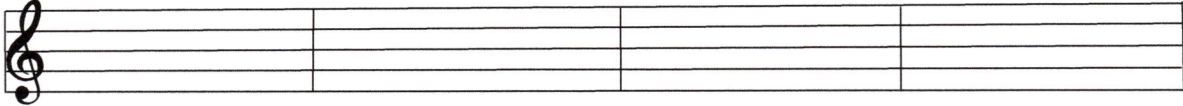

Chorus

B

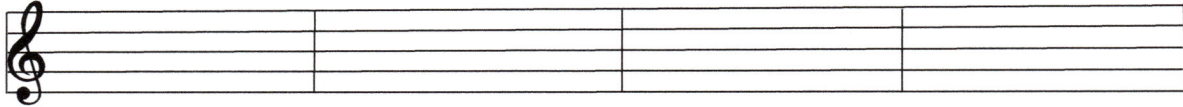

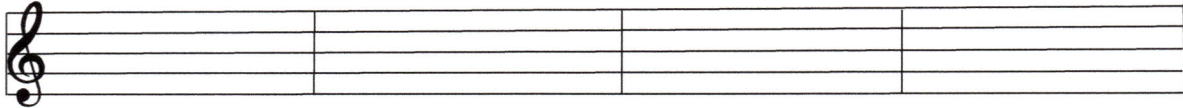

Bridge

C

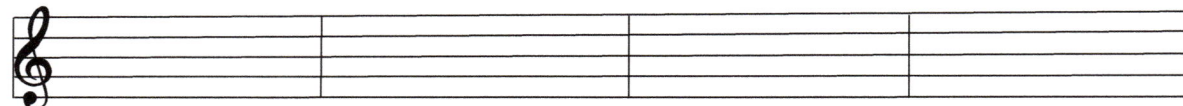

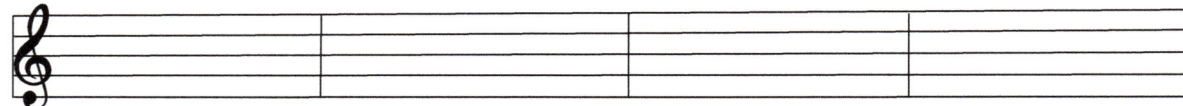

Chord Progressions

A

B

C

Song Structure

Lyrics

Verse 1

A1

_____
_____
_____
_____
_____
_____

Verse 2

A2

_____
_____
_____
_____
_____

Chorus

B

_____
_____
_____
_____
_____

Bridge

C

_____
_____
_____
_____
_____
_____

Inspiration

Mood

Checklist

- [ ] Song Written
- [ ] Pre-Production Complete
- [ ] Song recorded
- [ ] Song Mixed
- [ ] Song Mastered
- [ ] Album Art
- [ ] Copyright
- [ ] Meta-Data Complete
- [ ] Song Submitted to Distrokid
- [ ] Registered with PRO
- [ ] Recording Registered with SoundExchange
- [ ] Video Recorded
- [ ] Social Posts Scheduled
- [ ] Sent to fans
- [ ] Sent to Music Libraries
- [ ] Sent to Playlists

www.MusicAdvice.io

Rhythm and Melody

Verse

A

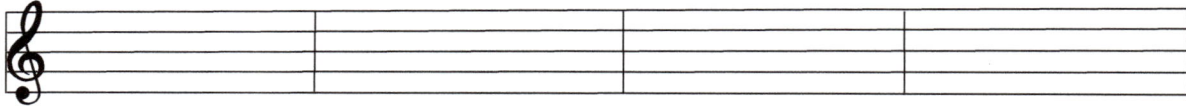

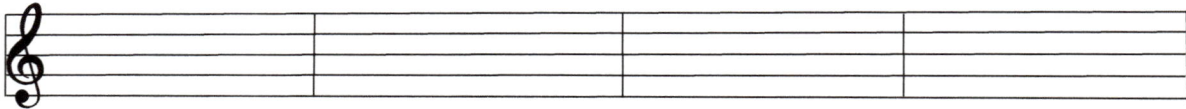

Chorus

B

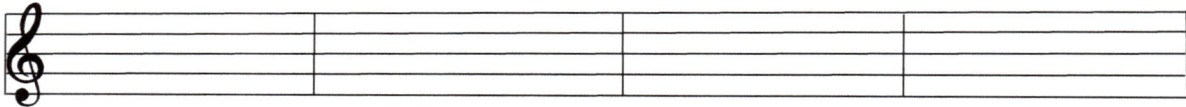

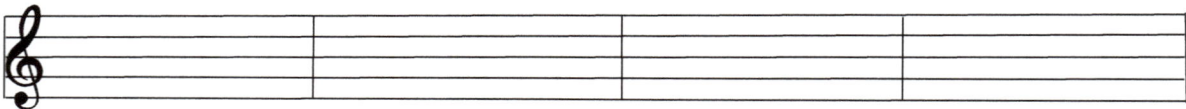

Bridge

C

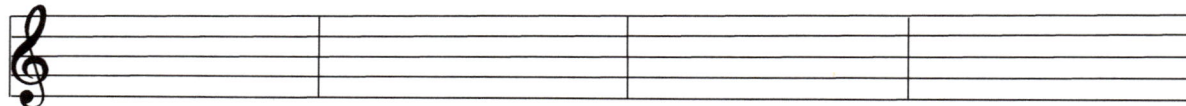

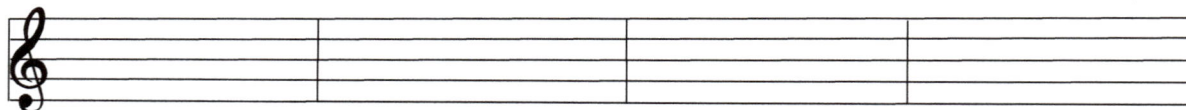

Chord Progressions

A

B

C

Song Structure

Lyrics

Verse 1

A1 _____
_____
_____
_____
_____
_____
_____
_____

Verse 2

A2 _____
_____
_____
_____
_____
_____

Chorus

B _____
_____
_____
_____
_____
_____

Bridge

C _____
_____
_____
_____
_____
_____
_____

Inspiration

Mood

Checklist

- [ ] Song Written
- [ ] Pre-Production Complete
- [ ] Song recorded
- [ ] Song Mixed
- [ ] Song Mastered
- [ ] Album Art
- [ ] Copyright
- [ ] Meta-Data Complete
- [ ] Song Submitted to Distrokid
- [ ] Registered with PRO
- [ ] Recording Registered with SoundExchange
- [ ] Video Recorded
- [ ] Social Posts Scheduled
- [ ] Sent to fans
- [ ] Sent to Music Libraries
- [ ] Sent to Playlists

www.MusicAdvice.io

Front

Rhythm and Melody

Verse

A

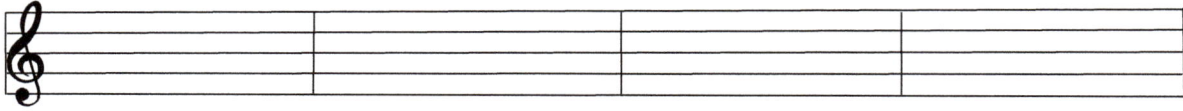

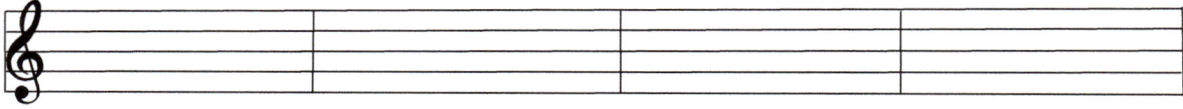

Chorus

B

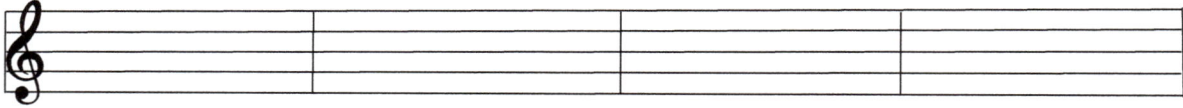

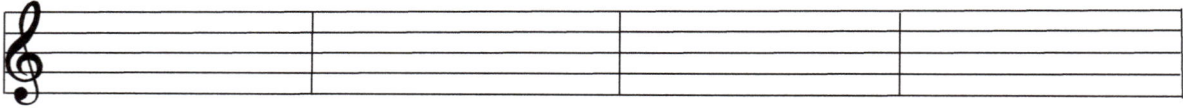

Bridge

C

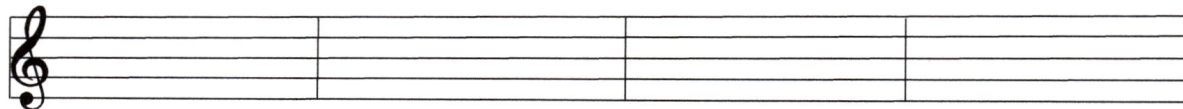

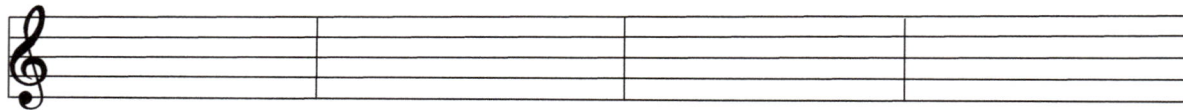

Chord Progressions

A

B

C

Song Structure

Lyrics

Verse 1

A1

_____
_____
_____
_____
_____
_____

Verse 2

A2

_____
_____
_____
_____
_____
_____

Chorus

B

_____
_____
_____
_____
_____
_____

Bridge

C

_____
_____
_____
_____
_____
_____

Inspiration

Mood

Checklist

- [ ] Song Written
- [ ] Pre-Production Complete
- [ ] Song recorded
- [ ] Song Mixed
- [ ] Song Mastered
- [ ] Album Art
- [ ] Copyright
- [ ] Meta-Data Complete
- [ ] Song Submitted to Distrokid
- [ ] Registered with PRO
- [ ] Recording Registered with SoundExchange
- [ ] Video Recorded
- [ ] Social Posts Scheduled
- [ ] Sent to fans
- [ ] Sent to Music Libraries
- [ ] Sent to Playlists

www.MusicAdvice.io

Rhythm and Melody

Verse

A

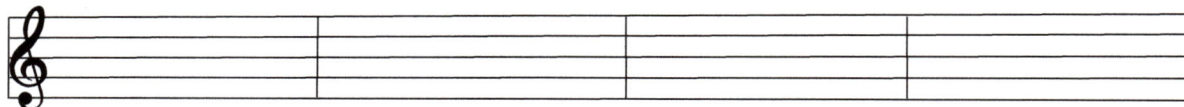

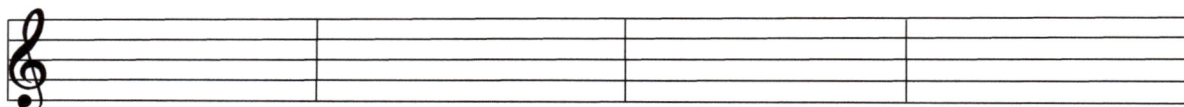

Chorus

B

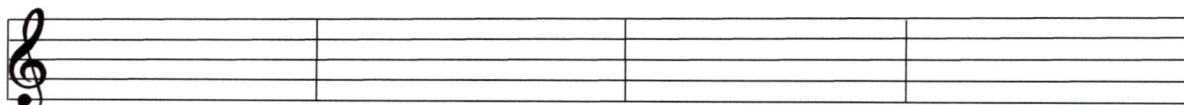

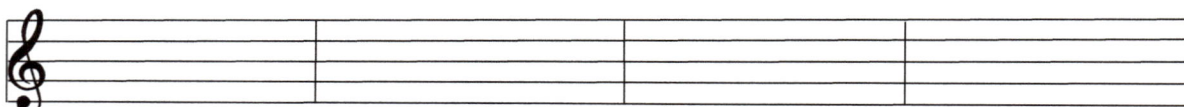

Bridge

C

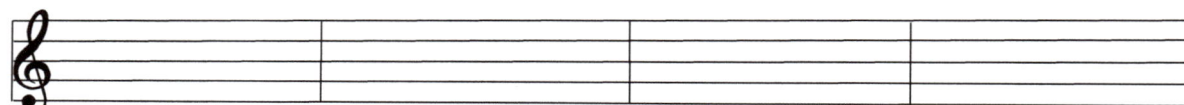

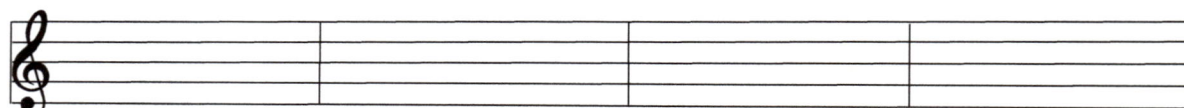

Chord Progressions

A

B

C

Song Structure

Lyrics

Verse 1

A1

_____

_____

_____

_____

_____

_____

_____

Verse 2

A2

_____

_____

_____

_____

_____

_____

Chorus

B

_____

_____

_____

_____

_____

_____

Bridge

C

_____

_____

_____

_____

_____

_____

_____

Inspiration

Mood

Checklist

- [ ] Song Written
- [ ] Pre-Production Complete
- [ ] Song recorded
- [ ] Song Mixed
- [ ] Song Mastered
- [ ] Album Art
- [ ] Copyright
- [ ] Meta-Data Complete
- [ ] Song Submitted to Distrokid
- [ ] Registered with PRO
- [ ] Recording Registered with SoundExchange
- [ ] Video Recorded
- [ ] Social Posts Scheduled
- [ ] Sent to fans
- [ ] Sent to Music Libraries
- [ ] Sent to Playlists

Rhythm and Melody

Verse

A

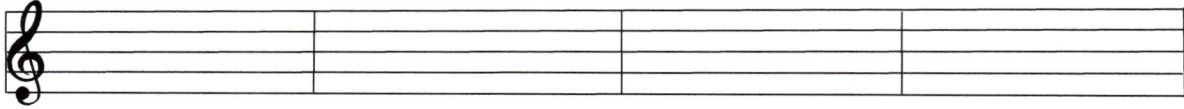

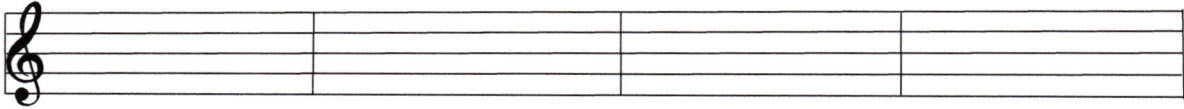

Chorus

B

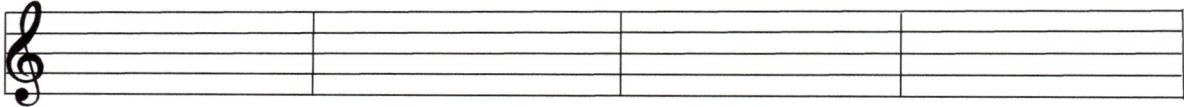

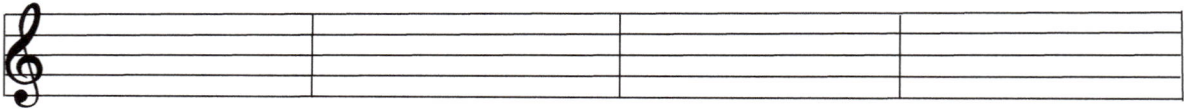

Bridge

C

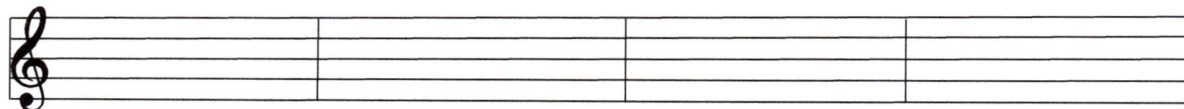

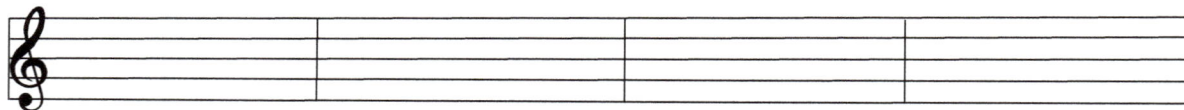

Chord Progressions

A

B

C

Song Structure

Lyrics

Verse 1

A1

_____

_____

_____

_____

_____

_____

_____

_____

Verse 2

A2

_____

_____

_____

_____

_____

_____

Chorus

B

_____

_____

_____

_____

_____

_____

Bridge

C

_____

_____

_____

_____

_____

Inspiration

Mood

Checklist

- [ ] Song Written
- [ ] Pre-Production Complete
- [ ] Song recorded
- [ ] Song Mixed
- [ ] Song Mastered
- [ ] Album Art
- [ ] Copyright
- [ ] Meta-Data Complete
- [ ] Song Submitted to Distrokid
- [ ] Registered with PRO
- [ ] Recording Registered with SoundExchange
- [ ] Video Recorded
- [ ] Social Posts Scheduled
- [ ] Sent to fans
- [ ] Sent to Music Libraries
- [ ] Sent to Playlists

www.MusicAdvice.io

Rhythm and Melody

Verse

A

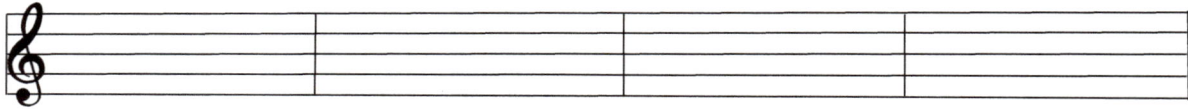

Chorus

B

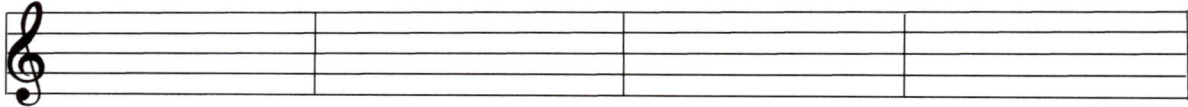

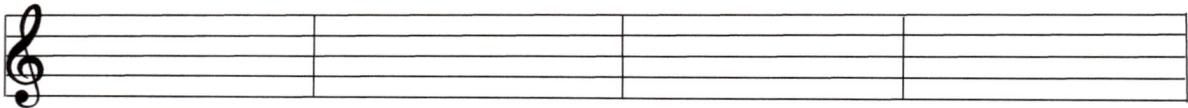

Bridge

C

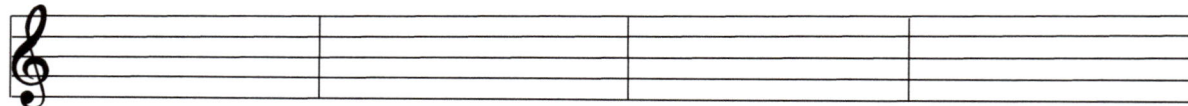

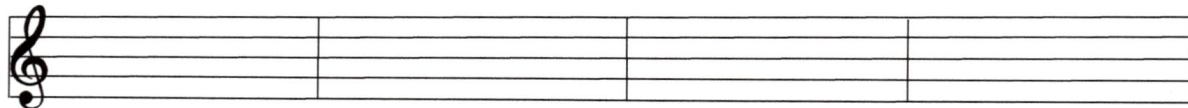

Chord Progressions

A

B

C

Song Structure

Lyrics

Verse 1

A1
_____
_____
_____
_____
_____
_____
_____
_____

Verse 2

A2
_____
_____
_____
_____
_____
_____
_____

Chorus

B
_____
_____
_____
_____
_____
_____

Bridge

C
_____
_____
_____
_____
_____
_____

Inspiration

Mood

Checklist

- [ ] Song Written
- [ ] Pre-Production Complete
- [ ] Song recorded
- [ ] Song Mixed
- [ ] Song Mastered
- [ ] Album Art
- [ ] Copyright
- [ ] Meta-Data Complete
- [ ] Song Submitted to Distrokid
- [ ] Registered with PRO
- [ ] Recording Registered with SoundExchange
- [ ] Video Recorded
- [ ] Social Posts Scheduled
- [ ] Sent to fans
- [ ] Sent to Music Libraries
- [ ] Sent to Playlists

Rhythm and Melody

Verse

A

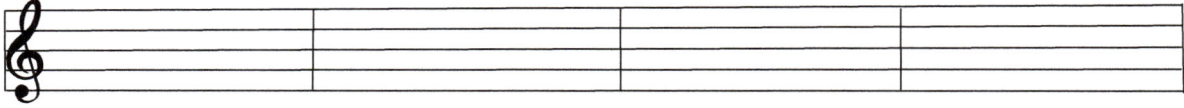

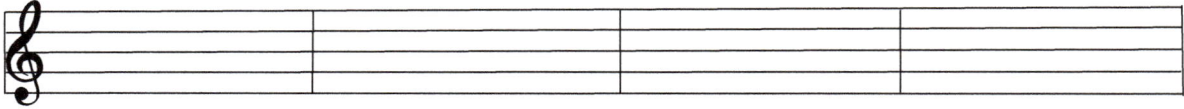

Chorus

B

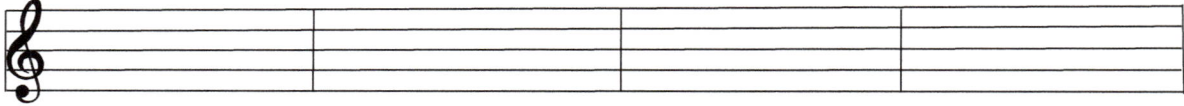

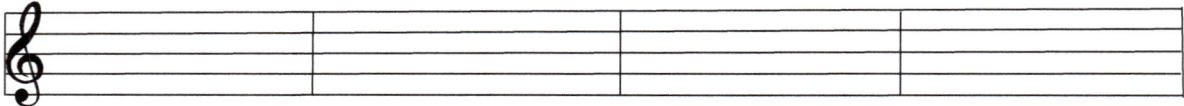

Bridge

C

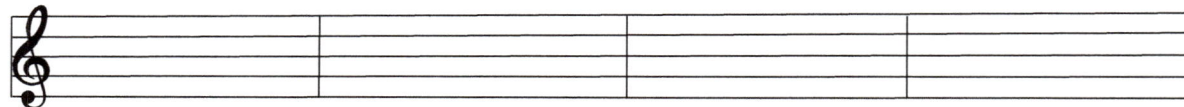

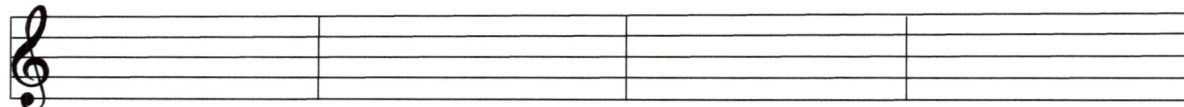

Chord Progressions

A

B

C

Song Structure

Lyrics

Verse 1

A1
_____
_____
_____
_____
_____
_____
_____

Verse 2

A2
_____
_____
_____
_____
_____
_____

Chorus

B
_____
_____
_____
_____
_____

Bridge

C
_____
_____
_____
_____
_____
_____
_____

Inspiration

Mood

Checklist

- [ ] Song Written
- [ ] Pre-Production Complete
- [ ] Song recorded
- [ ] Song Mixed
- [ ] Song Mastered
- [ ] Album Art
- [ ] Copyright
- [ ] Meta-Data Complete
- [ ] Song Submitted to Distrokid
- [ ] Registered with PRO
- [ ] Recording Registered with SoundExchange
- [ ] Video Recorded
- [ ] Social Posts Scheduled
- [ ] Sent to fans
- [ ] Sent to Music Libraries
- [ ] Sent to Playlists

www.MusicAdvice.io

Rhythm and Melody

Verse

A

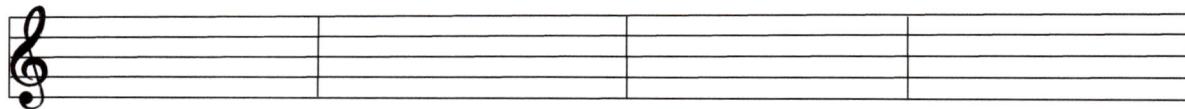

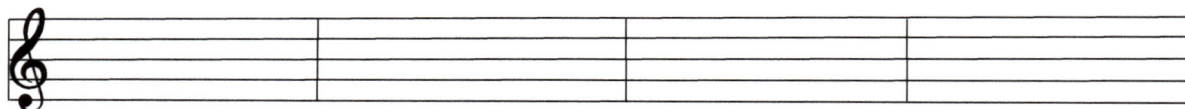

Chorus

B

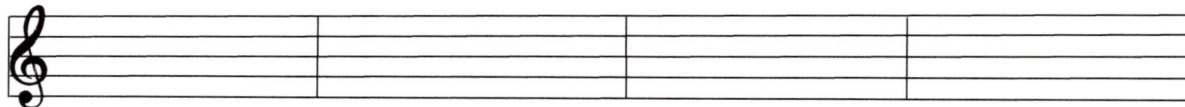

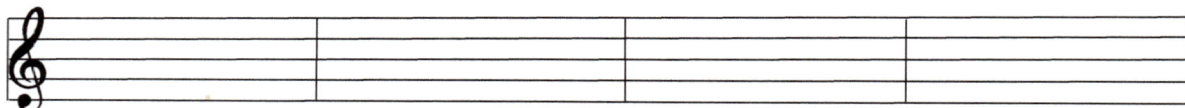

Bridge

C

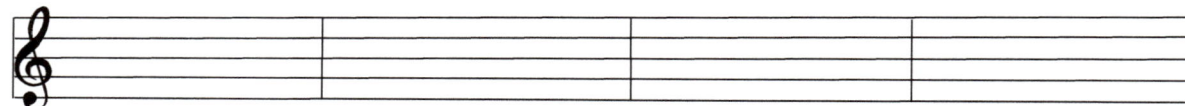

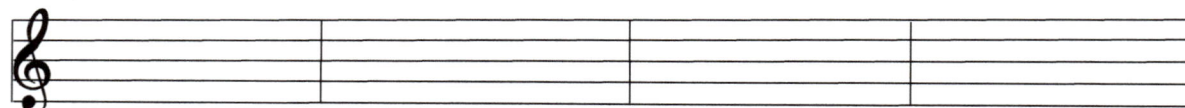

Chord Progressions

A

B

C

Song Structure

Lyrics

Verse 1

A1

_____
_____
_____
_____
_____
_____
_____

Verse 2

A2

_____
_____
_____
_____
_____
_____

Chorus

B

_____
_____
_____
_____
_____

Bridge

C

_____
_____
_____
_____
_____
_____

Inspiration

Mood

Checklist

- [ ] Song Written
- [ ] Pre-Production Complete
- [ ] Song recorded
- [ ] Song Mixed
- [ ] Song Mastered
- [ ] Album Art
- [ ] Copyright
- [ ] Meta-Data Complete
- [ ] Song Submitted to Distrokid
- [ ] Registered with PRO
- [ ] Recording Registered with SoundExchange
- [ ] Video Recorded
- [ ] Social Posts Scheduled
- [ ] Sent to fans
- [ ] Sent to Music Libraries
- [ ] Sent to Playlists

Song Title _____   Date _____

Rhythm and Melody

Verse

A

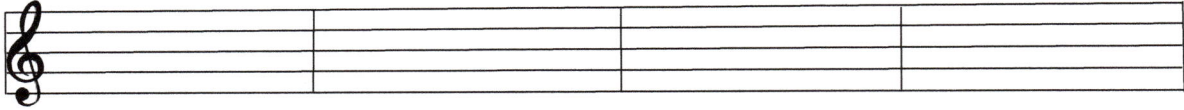

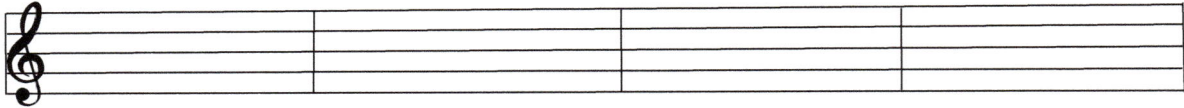

Chorus

B

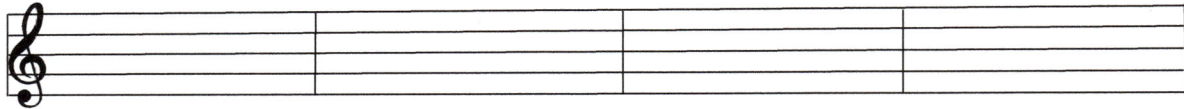

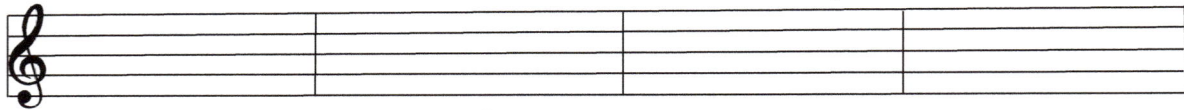

Bridge

C

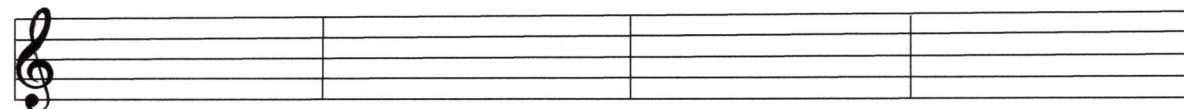

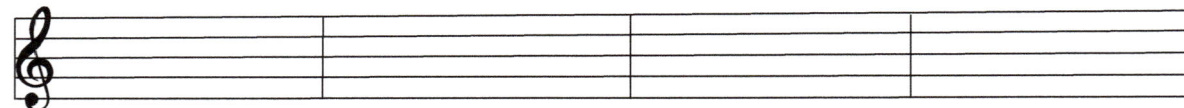

Chord Progressions

A

B

C

Song Structure

Back

Lyrics

Verse 1

A1

_____
_____
_____
_____
_____
_____
_____

Verse 2

A2

_____
_____
_____
_____
_____
_____

Chorus

B

_____
_____
_____
_____
_____
_____

Bridge

C

_____
_____
_____
_____
_____
_____
_____

Inspiration

Mood

Checklist

- [ ] Song Written
- [ ] Pre-Production Complete
- [ ] Song recorded
- [ ] Song Mixed
- [ ] Song Mastered
- [ ] Album Art
- [ ] Copyright
- [ ] Meta-Data Complete
- [ ] Song Submitted to Distrokid
- [ ] Registered with PRO
- [ ] Recording Registered with SoundExchange
- [ ] Video Recorded
- [ ] Social Posts Scheduled
- [ ] Sent to fans
- [ ] Sent to Music Libraries
- [ ] Sent to Playlists

www.MusicAdvice.io

Rhythm and Melody

Verse

A

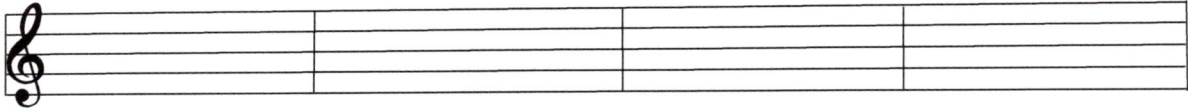

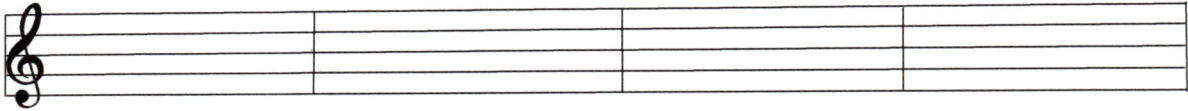

Chorus

B

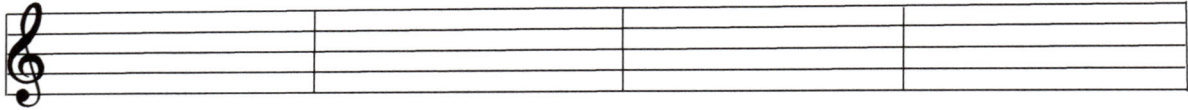

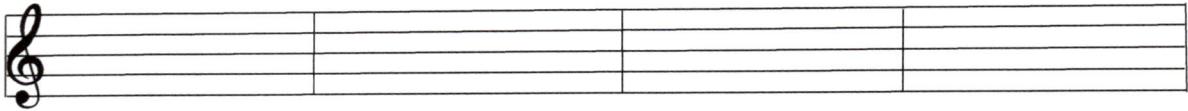

Bridge

C

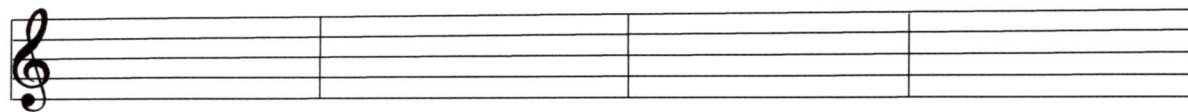

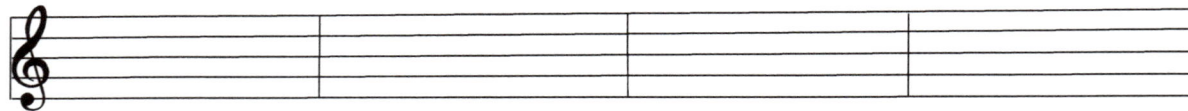

Chord Progressions

A

B

C

Song Structure

www.ingramcontent.com/pod-product-compliance
Lightning Source LLC
Chambersburg PA
CBHW040932050426

42334CB00050B/87